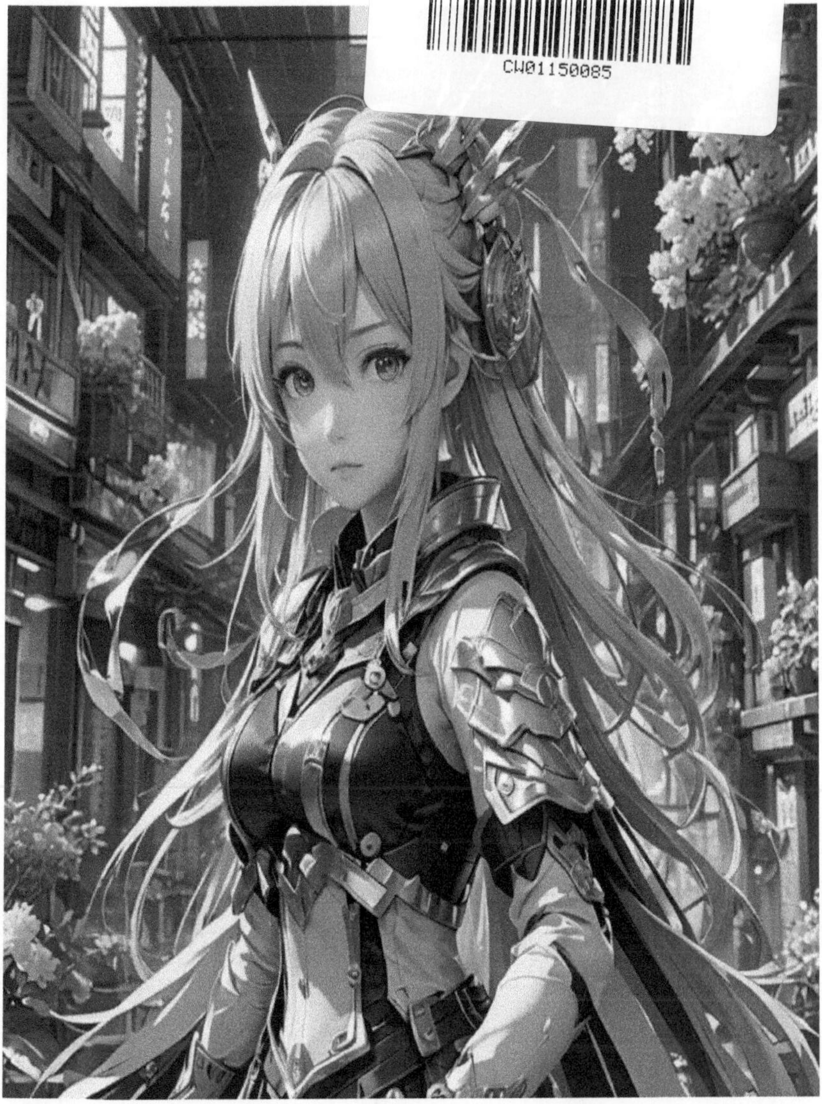

Streams of Prosperity
Crafting Your Online Income Assets
by
David Holman

Copyright 2024 David Holman. All rights reserved.

No part of this book may be reproduced in any form or by any electronic or mechanical means including information storage and retrieval systems, without permission in writing from the author. The only exception is by a reviewer, who may quote short excerpts in a review.

Although the author and publisher have made every effort to ensure that the information in this book was correct at press time, the author and publisher do not assume and hereby disclaim any liability to any party for any loss, damage, or disruption caused by errors or omissions, whether such errors or omissions result from negligence, accident, or any other cause.

This publication is designed to provide accurate and authoritative information with regard to the subject matter covered. It is sold with the understanding that the publisher is not engaged in rendering professional services. If legal advice or other expert assistance is required, the services of a competent professional should be sought.

The fact that an organization or website is referred to in this work as a citation and/or a potential source of further information does not mean that the author or the publisher endorses the information the organization or website may provide or recommendations it may make.

Please remember that Internet websites listed in this work may have changed or disappeared between when this work was written and when it is read.

Streams of Prosperity: Crafting Your Online Income Assets

Contents

Introduction

Chapter 1: Understanding Online Income Streams

Exploring the Digital Landscape

The Benefits of Income Diversification

Chapter 2: Building Your Digital Foundation

Selecting the Right Platforms

Creating an Effective Online Presence

Chapter 3: Blogging for Profit

Monetization Strategies for Blogs

Creating Compelling Content

Chapter 4: E-Commerce Essentials

Setting Up an Online Store

Effective Product Marketing

Chapter 5: Affiliate Marketing Success

Choosing Profitable Programs

Maximizing Affiliate Earnings

Chapter 6: Creating and Selling Digital Products

Types of Digital Products

Pricing and Distribution Strategies

Chapter 7: Navigating the World of Freelancing

Identifying Niche Skills

Building a Diverse Client Base

Chapter 8: Investing in Online Real Estate

Understanding Domain and Website Flipping

Evaluating Profitable Investments

Chapter 9: Leveraging Social Media for Income

Monetizing Social Media Platforms

Building and Engaging Your Audience

Chapter 10: Unlocking the Potential of Online Courses

Designing Engaging Course Content

Marketing Your Online Course

Chapter 11: Exploring Passive Income Opportunities

Automation in Digital Ventures

Revenue Streams Without Constant Attention

Chapter 12: Scaling and Sustaining Your Income Streams

Analyzing Growth Opportunities

Long-Term Strategies for Sustained Success

Conclusion

Appendix A: Resources for Online Entrepreneurs

Introduction

The digital landscape offers a treasure trove of opportunities for those daring enough to explore. In the age of connectivity, the potential to carve out a sustainable income stream online is not just a pipe dream—it's an attainable goal. You'll soon discover that today's digital age is not just about browsing and social networking; it's a fertile ground for those ready to cultivate diverse income streams. This book is your guide, whether you're an aspiring entrepreneur, a freelancer, or someone hungry to diversify your income. Packed with strategies, insights, and motivational guidance, it sets you on a path to harness online possibilities.

You're standing at the edge of a vast horizon, one filled with endless possibilities. The leap from traditional employment or reliance on a single income stream to the diverse world of digital income is both thrilling and daunting. It's akin to moving to a foreign country, where the language and customs are different, but the promise of a better life beckons. This book aims to be your roadmap in this new terrain, an atlas guiding you towards financial independence and creative fulfillment in the digital world.

Understanding the dynamics of digital income can seem overwhelming at first. But take heart—this book breaks down the complexities into manageable strategies and actions. You'll learn to identify and evaluate different online income streams, allowing you to choose those that align with your skills and passions. This isn't merely a manual; it's an empowerment tool designed to inspire action and instill confidence in your journey.

The world is rapidly shifting, and adaptability has become a cornerstone of success. No longer are we confined to traditional career paths or local markets. The global marketplace is at your fingertips, with countless niches waiting to be explored. As we embark on this journey, consider the possibilities: imagine supporting your lifestyle with income from blogging, e-commerce, affiliate marketing, or even creating and selling digital products. Each chapter is crafted to deepen your understanding, step by step, unveiling the layers of online entrepreneurship.

But why now? Why pivot to online income streams? The answer is multifaceted. First, diversification safeguards you against financial downturns. By cultivating multiple income streams, you're not placing all your eggs in one basket. You'll be equipped to withstand changes in the economy, industry-specific shifts, and personal career transitions. Income diversification in the digital realm frees you from dependency, empowering you to dictate your financial future.

Moreover, the flexibility of online work cannot be overstated. Imagine a lifestyle not chained to a nine-to-five schedule. Picture crafting your workday around your needs and passions, whether that means working from a cozy home office or a bustling café halfway around the world. The digital economy heralds autonomy, and with it, the freedom to build a life on your terms. It's this combination of flexibility and diversification that marks the digital landscape as a truly transformative opportunity.

As we delve into the realms of blogging, e-commerce, affiliate marketing, and more, remember that sustainability is our ultimate goal. It's about building income streams that not only flourish today but continue to prosper tomorrow. This book emphasizes long-term strategies over short-lived successes, guiding you toward building a digital foundation that withstands market changes and growing competition.

It's important to address a common misconception: the online world doesn't automatically equate to overnight success. Much like traditional businesses, building a sustainable income online requires dedication, persistence, and a clear strategy. Yet, for those willing to learn and adapt, the rewards can be profound. From seizing control over your financial destiny to achieving greater work-life balance, the impact of mastering online income streams can transform lives.

Empathy is woven throughout these pages because we understand the challenges inherent in making this leap. Many have walked this path before you, each facing their own fears, setbacks, and triumphs. The knowledge that others have tread this way offers solace and inspiration, encouraging you to step beyond doubt and into action.

The journey to creating sustainable online income is a personal one, shaped by individual skills, passions, and circumstances. What works for one may not work for another, and that's where personalized strategies come into play. This book encourages you to lean into your unique strengths, offering a variety of pathways to consider and customize as you see fit.

The world is at an inflection point, one where entrepreneurial spirit and digital innovation hold the keys to boundless potential. You're not just readers; you're pioneers at the forefront of this digital transformation. The tools, techniques, and mindsets shared within these pages are your companions on this transformative journey. As you turn these pages, allow yourself to dream, plan, and execute a vision of financial stability and creative freedom online.

As we begin, embrace the mindset of a lifelong learner. The digital landscape evolves rapidly, and continuous learning will be your ally in staying ahead. Each chapter offers a blend of theory and practice, encouraging you to engage actively with the content and apply it to your unique context. This balance of motivation and instruction empowers you to not just absorb information but translate it into meaningful action.

Welcome to a new beginning—a pathway to financial independence and flexibility you've imagined. This isn't solely about creating income; it's about crafting a life aligned with your values and aspirations. It's about empowerment and the promise of a future where you're in control. With commitment and vision, the digital world is truly your oyster. Let's unlock its potential, one strategic step at a time.

Chapter 1: Understanding Online Income Streams

In today's interconnected world, online income streams have become a beacon of opportunity for those seeking financial independence and flexibility. As you set foot on this digital journey, it's crucial to first understand the lay of the land. The digital ecosystem is vast and ever-changing, offering countless ways to generate income—from freelancing on the side to building a full-fledged digital business. But where does one begin, and how can you leverage these opportunities to not only gain financial stability but also thrive?

Let's start by examining the online income landscape. At its core, the digital economy encompasses a variety of platforms and opportunities, each with its own unique characteristics and challenges. You might choose to earn through traditional means like e-commerce and blogging or delve into more contemporary avenues such as affiliate marketing and online courses. The beauty of online income streams is their adaptability; they can be tailored to fit your skills, interests, and lifestyle. Yet, this flexibility requires a strategic approach to unlock their full potential.

One of the most significant benefits of cultivating multiple online income streams is diversification. Income diversification isn't just a financial buzzword; it's a powerful tool that can protect you from market volatility and economic downturns. By not putting all your eggs in one basket, you create a safety net, ensuring financial stability even when one stream underperforms. Think of it as planting a garden—variety increases the chance of a bountiful harvest, even if some crops don't fare as well in a particular season.

Yet, understanding these streams is more than knowing about the opportunities themselves; it involves a mindset shift. Embracing the digital landscape often means breaking away from traditional employment norms. It's about recognizing that success can come from a series of small, consistent actions rather than a single grand gesture. Each income stream you build is a stepping stone towards greater independence and control over your financial future. This new perspective opens doors to creativity, innovation, and empowerment.

However, just grasping the potential isn't enough—you need a clear direction. Begin by assessing your current assets: your skills, available time, and initial capital. Each of these plays a crucial role in determining which online income streams are most viable for you. Some ventures might require a financial investment upfront, while others demand more of your time and creativity. By aligning your strengths with the right opportunities, you'll set the stage for a successful foray into the digital market.

It's equally important to keep learning and adapting. The digital realm is known for its rapid advancements; what works well today might not be as effective tomorrow. Stay informed on industry trends, technological developments, and consumer behaviors. This ongoing education is your compass, guiding you through unknown waters and helping you pivot when necessary. Remember, adaptability is a key trait of successful entrepreneurs in an ever-evolving online world.

Finally, nurture your entrepreneurial spirit with patience and perseverance. Building online income streams isn't an overnight endeavor; it requires time, effort, and sometimes, trial and error. There will be setbacks along the way, but viewing them as learning experiences rather than failures can propel you forward. Celebrate the small victories and keep your eyes on the long-term goal: a sustainable, diverse portfolio of income streams that secure your financial future.

As you prepare to delve deeper into the specifics of each domain later in this book, keep in mind that the journey is yours to shape. With an understanding of the digital landscape and the benefits of diversification, you're better equipped to chase your own online income journey. Embrace the challenges, leverage your strengths, and keep moving forward. There's a world of potential waiting to be unlocked, and it starts with understanding.

Exploring the Digital Landscape

Diving into the digital landscape presents a wealth of opportunities that have redefined how we think about generating income. This vast and ever-changing environment isn't just a technological marvel; it's a frontier that can fuel your entrepreneurial aspirations. A realm where creativity and strategy blend seamlessly to offer a myriad of paths for aspiring entrepreneurs, freelancers, and anyone looking to diversify their income streams online.

In recent years, the digital realm has evolved far beyond simple e-commerce. Today, it encompasses everything from virtual services and subscription models to content creation and digital investments. No longer confined to office cubicles or brick-and-mortar stores, you're now empowered to explore innovative concepts and turn them into viable business models from anywhere in the world. This flexibility means you can adapt quickly to changing market demands and personal circumstances.

The first step in navigating this digital landscape requires understanding the wide array of potential online income streams. With the internet as your marketplace, the opportunities are limitless, yet not without challenge. Each path provides its unique benefits and hurdles. Your task is to assess which fits align best with your skills, interests, and goals, thus laying down a robust foundation upon which to build your digital ventures.

The digital landscape thrives on innovation. Think about the rise of influencers on social media platforms, whose personal brands have garnered them not just fame but lucrative sponsorship deals and product lines. Or consider the emergence of platform-exclusive content, where creatives offer paid memberships for exclusive access to premium content. These are just glimpses of how technology has transformed traditional business paradigms through new, dynamic portals of opportunity.

So, how exactly do you pinpoint the right opportunities for yourself in this landscape?

This starts with self-assessment and market research. Determine where your passions intersect with skills and market needs. Online tools and communities can be invaluable in providing insights and data about potential markets. Joining online forums or networks can help you gauge demand and competition and understand the nuances of your chosen field. This kind of background work offers a strategic advantage when carving out your niche.

But beware—*the same versatility that makes the digital landscape enticing can also be its trap.* The lure of easy money has led many to jump from one trend to the next, often abandoning half-built ventures along the way. Sustainable success comes from perseverance and strategically choosing which trends to embrace. Staying informed and adaptable is crucial, of course, but the most successful entrepreneurs are those who balance innovation with consistency.

Empathy plays a surprising role in exploiting this landscape. Successful entrepreneurs often focus not just on profit but on the value they can provide to their audience. Whether through solving a problem, providing entertainment, or delivering a service, being in tune with your audience's needs can set you apart in the digital world. Customers who feel valued and understood tend to be loyal and can become evangelists for your brand, multiplying your reach via word-of-mouth in the digital realm.

Moreover, collaboration in the digital space shouldn't be underestimated. With technology bridging the gap across continents, partnerships now transcend geographic boundaries. Whether teaming up with other influencers, joining affiliate programs, or co-creating content, collaboration can amplify your efforts exponentially. The shared expertise and extended networks that come with collaborations can offer fresh perspectives and open doors to audiences that might've otherwise remained inaccessible.

As you plot your course within this digital ecosystem, focus on creating multiple income streams. Diversification doesn't just maximize potential earnings; it also acts as a safety net. Should one avenue encounter a downturn, others might flourish, providing stability. The digital landscape is rife with options, from affiliate marketing and e-books to virtual consulting and app creation.

Stay vigilant and informed about emerging technologies and platforms technologies like blockchain and artificial intelligence are continually transforming online opportunities, offering new avenues previously unimaginable. Embracing these changes early can provide a substantial edge over latecomers. While no one can predict the future, positioning yourself as a learner can lead to pioneering opportunities.

Finally, remember that exploration is an ongoing process. The digital landscape is ever-evolving, with new trends and platforms constantly reshaping the possibilities. It might feel overwhelming at times, but it's also immensely exciting. Cherish the journey as much as you anticipate the destination, for it's this journey that will enrich your entrepreneurial practice and personal growth.

Through commitment, flexibility, and strategic action, the digital landscape can become your playground for success, offering endless possibilities for sustainable online income. Equip yourself with knowledge and courage, and the digital world just might surprise you with its bounty.

The Benefits of Income Diversification

In a world brimming with digital possibilities, the idea of sticking to just a single source of income seems antiquated. Imagine you're standing on a bridge built on a foundation of various pillars, each representing a different stream of income. If one pillar weakens, the others hold the bridge up, ensuring stability. This analogy encapsulates the essence of income diversification. By weaving a tapestry of multiple revenue streams, you not only fortify your financial standing but also unlock a suite of opportunities for growth and security.

At its core, income diversification reduces the financial instability that comes with relying on a singular revenue stream. Economic downturns, industry changes, or even shifts in consumer behavior can dramatically impact your primary income source. Spreading your earnings across different avenues acts as a buffer against these uncertainties. Think of it like a financial safety net—when one element of your income plan falters, others can fill the gap and maintain your overall earning power.

Beyond stability, diversifying your income can spark creativity and innovation. When you're involved in various sectors or projects, you continually learn and adapt, gaining new skills and knowledge. This exposure broadens your perspective, encouraging cross-disciplinary thinking and potentially opening doors to ventures you hadn't previously considered. It's a bit like an artist who experiments with different mediums—each new experience enriches their craft and offers fresh layers of expression.

Moreover, diversifying your income streams taps into the burgeoning gig and online entrepreneurial economy. Today, myriad platforms provide the means to convert hobbies and skills into income-generating opportunities. From writing blogs to creating digital products or leveraging social media, the digital landscape offers endless possibilities. Choosing a mix that aligns with your interests and expertise can turn work into a passion project, making the pursuit of money an enjoyable endeavor rather than a task.

Financial diversification, however, isn't just about individual empowerment; it can be a stepping stone toward community support and economic impact. By exploring different income routes, you may find ways to invest in others, from hiring freelance talent to collaborating with entrepreneurs who share your vision. This collaborative spirit can foster a network of like-minded individuals who uplift each other, creating a ripple effect that extends beyond personal gain.

Nevertheless, it's essential to approach diversification strategically. Not every opportunity is worth pursuing. It's crucial to assess the viability and scalability of each potential income stream. A clear understanding of your strengths and market demands will guide you in selecting the most promising ventures. Here, careful planning and diligent research play pivotal roles. A well-thought-out strategy, akin to a seasoned chess player, can place you several steps ahead in the game of income diversification.

Additionally, diversifying can enhance your financial literacy. As you delve into different revenue models, you'll inevitably learn about budgeting, investment, and financial management. This accumulated knowledge empowers you to make informed choices, not just within your business endeavors but also in personal life decisions. The wisdom gained from diverse income streams offers resilience, allowing you to navigate both thriving and challenging economic landscapes.

There's also a psychological benefit to having income coming from various sources. It can alleviate the pressure and stress of depending on a single job or venture. The knowledge that your financial well-being doesn't hinge on one point of failure can be deeply reassuring. This peace of mind encourages a healthier work-life balance, giving you the freedom and flexibility to pursue what truly matters in life beyond the pursuit of income.

For those who are pondering when to begin diversifying, the answer is simple: there's no better time than now. The digital economy thrives on early adoption, and those who are proactive in exploring diverse earning avenues often have a competitive edge. Start by leveraging what you know while progressively expanding into areas you're passionate about or willing to learn more about. Keep in mind that even small streams can grow with time and dedication.

In conclusion, income diversification isn't just a prudent financial practice—it's a gateway to innovation, security, and personal growth. It allows you to harness the full potential of the digital age, opening new horizons while safeguarding against unpredictability. As you build and expand your array of online income streams, you're not just constructing a financial fortress; you're crafting a more fulfilling, dynamic life journey.

Chapter 2: Building Your Digital Foundation

Embarking on your journey through the digital landscape requires more than just enthusiasm; it necessitates a solid foundation upon which to build your future endeavors. Think of this foundation as the cornerstone of a skyscraper, enabling you to reach towering heights with stability and confidence. Establishing this base is crucial, giving you the tools, skills, and mindset necessary to navigate the complex world of online income streams.

Start by understanding that not all digital platforms are created equal. Every tool in your arsenal should serve a purpose, aligned with your goals and strengths. As you begin selecting platforms to support your ventures, consider both your audience and the type of content or products you wish to share. Some platforms excel in visual content, while others may be more text-oriented or suitable for video. Choose wisely, and always keep scalability in mind.

Building a digital foundation goes beyond just choosing the right tools; it's about creating an effective online presence. Imagine your online identity as your digital storefront—it should be visually appealing, memorable, and aligned with your brand message. This involves crafting a cohesive narrative that spans across platforms, enhancing the viewer's experience from the first click to the final conversion.

Your online presence should reflect authenticity and relatability. In a world saturated with content, authenticity shines through as a beacon for your audience. It's not just about sharing successes but also showing the human side of your journey, the bumps, and lessons along the way. Audiences connect with vulnerability and genuine stories.

Let's not underestimate the power of consistency in building your digital footprint. Regularly engaging with your audience through consistent content and interaction strengthens trust and fosters a community. Consistency doesn't mean repetition but rather maintaining a steady rhythm of value and engagement. It's this persistence that converts casual visitors into loyal followers and customers.

Moreover, as you establish your digital foundation, surround yourself with a network of support and inspiration. Seek out mentors, join forums, or engage in communities of like-minded individuals. The digital economy can be daunting, but you're not alone. There's immense strength in collaboration and learning from others' experiences. Knowledge shared is knowledge multiplied.

Remember, building your digital foundation is dynamic. The digital world evolves rapidly, demanding adaptability and continuous learning. Embrace change as an opportunity rather than a disruption. Stay informed about new trends and technologies, but remain grounded in the principles that define your brand. This balance is crucial in sustaining and expanding your digital foothold.

Patience is your silent partner in this journey. The process of building a digital foundation is not instantaneous. Like any good investment, it requires time and thoughtful nurturing. Celebrate small victories along the way, as each step fortifies your foundation. Persevere, and in time, the dividends of your efforts will become apparent, providing a stable base for future growth and success.

In conclusion, the bedrock of building a thriving digital enterprise lies in crafting a robust foundation. With the right platforms, an engaging online presence, authenticity, consistency, and a network of support, you're poised to navigate the exciting terrain of digital entrepreneurship. Remember, this foundation isn't just about the here and now—it's about carving pathways for continuous discovery and growth in the incredible world of online income potentials.

Selecting the Right Platforms

As you embark on your journey to build a robust digital foundation, one of the critical decisions you'll face is choosing the right platforms. This decision is akin to laying down the tracks for future success. The digital realm is a vast universe with countless platforms promising growth, visibility, and income. But how do you filter through all the noise to find the ideal spaces tailored to your unique goals and skills? Getting it right means the difference between sinking time into a black hole and building a space where your digital endeavors can thrive.

First and foremost, it's vital to have a clear understanding of your target audience. Who are they? What do they value? Where do they spend their time online? Platforms like Facebook, Instagram, LinkedIn, Twitter, and Pinterest each have distinct user demographics. For instance, LinkedIn might be your best bet if you're offering professional services or B2B products. In contrast, a lifestyle brand might flourish more on Instagram or Pinterest, which lean heavily into visual content.

Once you know where your audience hangs out, consider the nature of your content. Are you crafting long-form written content, or is your message better suited to short, punchy videos? Maybe you're skilled at crafting multimedia content that involves both video and imagery. Different platforms are designed to support various content types. Blogs or websites might suit in-depth articles, while platforms like TikTok or YouTube cater to those capable of engaging through dynamic visual storytelling.

Another consideration is the platform's monetization potential. Some platforms offer built-in monetization features, such as YouTube's ad revenue sharing or Instagram's shopping integration. Investigating these opportunities is crucial because they might align with your desired income streams. Keep in mind, however, that having a presence on a monetizable platform doesn't guarantee revenue. It's about strategically leveraging the tools available.

Platforms like Amazon, Etsy, and Shopify provide avenues for entrepreneurs focused on e-commerce. Each has its own ecosystem and user expectations, so research is paramount. Are you selling handmade crafts? Etsy's community might be more welcoming. If you're focusing on a broad market with diverse products, Amazon could offer access to a larger customer base. Shopify presents itself as a comprehensive toolset for those wanting to build a fully branded online store.

You should also be aware of platform shifts. The digital space evolves rapidly, and algorithms or policies can change overnight. Diversifying your platform presence can reduce the risk of sudden changes affecting your business. However, managing multiple platforms requires organization and strategic planning to avoid spreading yourself too thin.

Testing and adaptability are your allies. Start by investing time into a couple of platforms, focusing on gaining traction and understanding your audience's response. This approach also allows for experimentation with different content types and strategies. Pay attention to analytics to gain insights into what's working and what's not, and don't hesitate to pivot when necessary.

Furthermore, consider scalability. As your digital ventures grow, will the platforms you've chosen support increased demand and engagement? Ensuring the platforms can scale with you is essential for long-term success. Look for platforms with robust support services or communities that can assist during growth phases.

In conclusion, selecting the right platforms is a strategic exercise that requires understanding both your audience and your own strengths. It's about aligning your digital efforts with the right tools to pave the path toward sustainable online income. This decision is foundational because, when aligned effectively, the chosen platforms will act as catalysts, propelling you toward achieving your digital objectives with greater ease and efficiency.

Creating an Effective Online Presence

Welcome to a world where your digital footprint can be as powerful as a face-to-face handshake. In today's fast-paced digital landscape, creating an effective online presence isn't just a nice-to-have; it's a necessity. This chapter delves into the strategies, tools, and mindsets needed to build a presence that not only gets noticed but also drives the sustainable income you're striving to achieve.

First things first, your online presence is your brand's digital identity. It's what people find when they Google your name or business. Think of it as your digital calling card. A well-crafted online presence tells potential clients or customers who you are, what you do, and why you do it. It's about presenting yourself authentically while also being aware of the impression you leave behind.

Why is it so crucial? Well, an effective online presence can open doors to opportunities that would be unreachable otherwise. In an age where millions of voices clamor for attention, standing out can seem daunting. Yet, with the right approach, you don't have to shout to be heard. You can create a resonant presence that draws people in naturally.

At the core of your online presence is your personal brand. Think of it as the unique blend of skills, experiences, and passions that only you possess. Crafting a personal brand involves introspection and clarity—what do you want to be known for? What problems can you solve for your audience? Understanding these elements helps you convey a message that is uniquely yours.

Let's talk about consistency. Consistency is key in building trust. From the visual elements like your logo and website design to the tone of voice in your content, maintaining a cohesive and consistent message ensures that your audience knows what to expect. And in the world of online business, trust is tantamount to success.

Another critical component is authenticity. In an age filled with filters and façades, authenticity stands out. People are drawn to those who are genuine and transparent. Share your story, your challenges, and your victories. When your audience feels connected to your journey, they are more likely to become part of it by supporting your ventures and recommending you to others.

If you're serious about creating an effective online presence, investing in a professional website is a must. This is your home base, where potential clients can learn more about you and your offerings. Make it mobile-friendly, ensure fast load times, and design it with your target audience in mind. It should be easy to navigate yet rich with the information your audience craves.

Don't underestimate the power of content. Whether it's blog posts, videos, or podcasts, creating valuable content not only positions you as an authority in your niche but also drives organic traffic to your site. Content is a way to provide value upfront, establish credibility, and engage with your audience on a deeper level.

Social media platforms are not just tools for connection; they're powerful vehicles for personal branding and business growth. Dedicate time to identify which platforms resonate most with your audience. Maybe it's Instagram for visual storytelling, LinkedIn for professional networking, or even TikTok for reaching a younger demographic. The key is to be where your audience is and communicate in ways that they appreciate.

Engagement is another crucial aspect. An effective online presence is not a one-way street; it's about interaction. Respond to comments, engage in discussions, and make it a point to listen to your audience. This not only boosts your visibility but also builds a community around your brand.

Leveraging analytics can provide insights into what's working and what needs adjustment. Tools like Google Analytics or social media insights help track your progress and inform data-driven decisions.

Don't be afraid to try new strategies, but always be ready to pivot based on what the data tells you.

Finally, never stop learning. The digital world evolves rapidly, with new tools and trends emerging constantly. Stay updated by following industry leaders, participating in webinars, or even taking online courses. The more you learn, the better equipped you are to enhance your online presence and harness it for income-generation.

Building an effective online presence is a journey of self-discovery and external exploration. It's about crafting a digital identity that reflects your true self while meeting the needs and expectations of your audience. Embrace this process with creativity, authenticity, and consistency, and you'll build a foundation that not only supports your current goals but also propels you towards future success in the online landscape.

Chapter 3: Blogging for Profit

Blogs have long been a cornerstone of the digital world, serving as platforms for self-expression, information sharing, and, importantly, profit. The allure of blogging lies in its accessibility—practically anyone with an internet connection and a passion can start a blog. But transforming a blog into a money-making machine? That requires strategy, creativity, and persistence.

To embark on the journey of blogging for profit, one must first grasp the basics of monetization. There are multiple avenues to consider, each catering to different strengths and niches. Whether it's through advertising, sponsored content, or affiliate marketing, the key is to align your monetization strategy with your brand and audience.

Advertising is one of the most straightforward methods to generate income. Platforms like Google AdSense allow you to display ads relevant to your content and earn money when readers interact with them. However, don't be fooled into thinking it's an easy path to riches. Successful bloggers often cultivate significant traffic before seeing substantial ad revenue. Thus, patience and consistent quality are essential.

Sponsored content opens another promising avenue. Companies are keen to collaborate with bloggers who can convincingly promote their products to a dedicated readership. To attract such partnerships, it's crucial to build trust with your audience by maintaining authenticity and honesty in your content. Readers value authenticity over anything else in the content they consume daily.

The creation of compelling content is crucial, serving as the heartbeat of any successful blog. It's not just about churning out words to fill a page; it's about captivating your audience, addressing their pain points, and offering them value they won't find elsewhere. A mix of well-researched articles, personal stories, and visually engaging media can set your blog apart in a saturated market.

One effective approach is to lean into your unique perspective and voice. Remember, people don't just follow blogs for information; they subscribe to **experience the world through your lens**. By staying authentic and sharing your distinct worldview, you cultivate a loyal community eager to engage with your content.

Moreover, think of your blog posts as conversations rather than monologues. Engage your readers with questions, encourage comments, and foster a community vibe where ideas flow both ways. This interaction not only enriches the reader's experience but also sharpens your understanding of their needs, refining your content strategy.

Building a successful blog requires you to anticipate and adapt to trends. Digital landscapes shift constantly, and what captivates audiences today might not do so tomorrow. Keep a finger on the pulse of your industry and general online trends to ensure your content remains fresh and relevant. Being adaptable increases your resilience in the face of change.

Search Engine Optimization (SEO) plays a crucial role in your blog's visibility. It's not merely about sprinkling keywords throughout your content; it's a comprehensive strategy involving metadata, backlinks, and quality link-building. Successfully implemented, SEO can drive organic traffic to your site, increasing earnings potential without the constant need for paid advertising.

Once you've drawn readers in, don't let them slip away without exploring all your blog offers. Turn first-time visitors into recurring ones with techniques such as email newsletters and drip campaigns. A loyal readership not only boosts traffic over time but also amplifies your influence as a brand, making future monetization efforts more effective.

Finally, pacing yourself is essential on this journey. The idea of overnight success is often just that—an idea. Building a profitable blog is a gradual process requiring dedication, experimentation, and learning from failures. Take time to plan, execute, and reflect on each step you take, and remember that consistency is your ally in crafting a sustainable income stream.

By weaving together strategic monetization strategies, creating content that resonates, and engaging genuinely with your audience, you're not just building a blog; you're laying the foundation of an empowered and self-reliant venture. The digital landscape offers ample opportunities, but success hinges on your willingness to seize and shape them to suit your passion and purpose. Keep persisting, keep evolving, and embrace the potential that blogging holds for profitable growth.

Monetization Strategies for Blogs

Imagine your blog as a digital garden. As with any garden, you need to tend to it seriously if you want it to bloom with financial success. Monetizing a blog involves more than just planting seeds of content and hoping for the best. It's about choosing the right mix of strategies tailored to fit your blog's unique soil.

First, let's talk about advertising. It's one of the most traditional ways to generate income from blogging. Display ads, whether incorporated through Google AdSense or direct advertising deals, can subtly blend into your blog's landscape. Every click and page view can contribute to an income stream that's both reliable and scalable. However, the key here is balance. You don't want your blog to feel overrun with ads, which could deter your audience. Instead, strategically place them where they'll attract attention without overwhelming your readers.

Affiliate marketing is another potent tool in your monetization toolkit. By promoting products or services relevant to your audience, you can earn commissions on sales generated through your recommendations. The trick? Authenticity and transparency. Readers are more likely to click an affiliate link if they trust your opinion. So, ensure your endorsements genuinely align with your content and provide real value to your audience.

Sponsored content is akin to hosting guest plants in your garden. Brands pay you to weave their message into your blog, often in the form of a post or review. This method allows you to maintain the creative freedom of your content while benefiting financially. Carefully vet potential sponsors to ensure they're a good fit for your audience's expectations. Your audience's trust is your most valuable asset, so nurture it by staying true to your voice and values.

For bloggers with a knack for selling, merchandise can be an exciting monetization path. Think about branded products that resonate with your audience, whether it's a line of t-shirts, mugs, or exclusive digital downloads. Platforms like Etsy or Shopify make it easier than ever to manage and sell physical products. Meanwhile, Patreon or Ko-fi can help with offering exclusive digital items or memberships, encouraging your most loyal followers to support your work directly.

Email marketing shouldn't be overlooked. Building a loyal subscriber base allows you to tap into a dedicated portion of your audience regularly. Through newsletters, you can market your products, update readers on new blog posts, and seamlessly integrate affiliate links or sponsored content. An engaged email list can become one of your most predictable sources of income, especially when nurtured with compelling, valuable content.

Courses or workshops related to your blog's niche can transform your readers into students. If you're an expert in your field, sharing that knowledge through structured learning experiences can be highly lucrative. Your blog can serve as both a marketing platform and a part of the curriculum, inviting loyal readers to deepen their expertise under your guidance.

Membership sites work well for those with a dedicated following. By creating a subscription model, you provide exclusive content or perks to members who support you financially. This strategy not only creates a steady income stream but also fosters a sense of community among your most engaged readers.

Leveraging social media amplification complements your monetization efforts. Each blog post has the potential to go viral or reach new audiences if shared effectively across platforms. Social media contests or collaborations with other bloggers can also drive traffic back to your blog, amplifying your monetization strategies organically.

It's crucial to analyze and adjust your strategies regularly. The digital landscape constantly evolves, and what works today might not tomorrow. Use analytics tools to track what's driving revenue and what's not. Based on these insights, don't be afraid to pivot or experiment with new methods.

Monetization strategies for blogs are not one-size-fits-all. Tailoring your approach to fit your unique voice and audience is critical for sustainable success. With dedication and a strategic mindset, your blog can indeed become a blossoming business venture, where each post serves as a stepping stone towards your entrepreneurial goals.

Creating Compelling Content

Creating compelling content is at the heart of a successful blogging strategy. When it comes to blogging for profit, compelling content isn't just about writing well; it's about connecting with your audience on a deeper level. It's about understanding their needs, desires, and pain points. Great content resonates, drawing readers in and keeping them engaged. That engagement translates into higher traffic, better monetization opportunities, and a loyal reader base that returns time and again.

But how do you create content that captivates and converts? First, you must know your target audience like the back of your hand. Get into their heads—what are they searching for? What keeps them up at night? Whether you're addressing aspiring entrepreneurs, freelancers, or anyone exploring the digital landscape, tailor your content to speak directly to their experiences and future aspirations. This isn't about guessing; it's about dedicating time to research and understanding. Remember, empathy goes a long way in content creation.

Consistency is key when building a successful blog. Consistent posting not only builds anticipation and loyalty but also signals to search engines that your site is active and relevant. However, this doesn't mean flooding your blog with mediocre posts. Quality should always trump quantity. Aim for a cadence that you can manage without sacrificing the value of your content. Weekly, bi-weekly—find your rhythm and stick with it.

Storytelling is an art that every blogger must master. Humans are hardwired for stories. They stick in our minds, make us feel connected, and often drive us to take action. By weaving narratives into your content, you create an emotional bond with your readers. This doesn't mean every post has to be a personal essay, but using anecdotes and relatable scenarios can powerfully illustrate your points and make your message more memorable and impactful.

The language you use should vary based on your blog's niche and your target audience. A blog aimed at tech-savvy readers can indulge in jargon that a more general audience might find overwhelming. Tailor your tone, style, and vocabulary to fit your readers' familiarity with the topic. Incorporate humor, if it fits, or keep it strictly professional if that's what's expected. The goal is to speak their language, quite literally.

Another critical aspect of compelling content is delivering on the promises your headlines make. This isn't about clickbait; it's about crafting clear, intriguing titles that honestly reflect the content within. A strong headline can draw readers in, while unfulfilled promises can lead to distrust and disinterest. Don't just aim to attract clicks—aim to deliver substance that meets or exceeds your audience's expectations.

Incorporating multimedia elements like images, infographics, and videos can greatly enhance the appeal of your content. Visuals break up text, provide additional layers of context, and can make complex information more digestible. As you create, consider what format will serve your message best and enrich your reader's experience. Additionally, visuals can be a great way to engage with different learning styles and broaden your audience.

Search engine optimization (SEO) is a vital component of compelling content creation. While the algorithms are ever-changing, the essence remains the same: provide valuable, well-organized information. Use keywords judiciously, write engaging meta descriptions, and structure your posts with headers to improve readability and searchability. Don't get too bogged down chasing SEO trends, but keep best practices in mind as you write.

At its core, compelling content is all about creating value for your reader. This means offering insights, solutions, or inspiration that earn their trust and loyalty. Engage in conversation through reader comments and feedback, allowing you to refine your future posts to even better meet their needs. This two-way communication builds a community around your blog, transforming passive readers into active participants.

Finally, never underestimate the power of a strong call to action (CTA). Compelling content invariably nudges readers toward some form of engagement—be it leaving a comment, sharing a post, or clicking through to another link. CTAs should be clear, persuasive, and well-positioned without being intrusive or overly aggressive. Think of them as gentle invitations that guide your readers towards a meaningful interaction.

Remember, creating compelling content is an ongoing process. It requires both heart and strategy. Learn from each piece you craft, pay attention to the metrics that matter, and continuously adapt to engage your audience better. As your blog grows, so too will your understanding of what your readers crave from you. In this dynamic dance of content creation, aim to inspire, inform, and ultimately add value.

Chapter 4: E-Commerce Essentials

Embarking on the e-commerce journey is like opening a gateway to almost limitless possibilities. With the right mindset and tools, you can transform simple ideas into thriving online businesses. In the world of e-commerce, understanding the essentials can set you apart from simply participating in the digital marketplace to truly dominating it. This chapter will guide you through key components crucial to building and maintaining a successful online store.

At its core, e-commerce involves selling products or services over the internet, but there's more to it than meets the eye. It's about creating experiences, fostering connections, and building trust with your customers. Your online store is not just a digital shelf for products; it's an opportunity to tell a story, engage your audience, and meet their needs in unique and valuable ways.

First and foremost, setting up an online store effectively is all about choosing the right e-commerce platform. Today's market offers a variety of options like Shopify, WooCommerce, and BigCommerce, each catering to different needs and business scales. The best platform is one that aligns with your business model, budget, and technical proficiency. It's essential to consider scalability from the get-go because what works for a startup might not suffice as you grow.

Once you've settled on a platform, focus on your niche. Understanding your target market allows you to tailor your offerings and marketing strategies more precisely. An overlooked yet vital aspect is comprehensive product research. Knowing what sells, and more importantly, what your customers want, can make or break your venture. Engaging directly with potential customers for feedback and assessing competitors for inspiration provides valuable insights.

An exceptional online store doesn't just present products; it communicates value through aesthetics and ease of use. Design is much more than simple visuals. It's about creating an intuitive user experience where navigation feels seamless and encourages purchases. Clarity and simplicity in design can't be overstated. The fewer barriers you have, the more likely visitors will convert to customers.

The checkout process is another critical piece of the puzzle. It should be as simple and frictionless as possible. Shopping cart abandonment is an all-too-common issue in e-commerce, often due to a cumbersome checkout experience. Consider offering multiple payment options and ensure your site is mobile-friendly, as more and more transactions happen on mobile devices.

While having an attractive store is vital, it's equally important to have impactful product marketing strategies. Visibility reigns supreme in the digital age. Your marketing should be a delicate balance between storytelling and value proposition. It's about creating a message that resonates with customers and compels them to choose you over the competition. SEO, or search engine optimization, plays a crucial role in driving organic traffic to your store. Crafting detailed, keyword-rich product descriptions and blog content can improve your visibility on search engines like Google.

Social media is a formidable ally in your marketing arsenal. Platforms like Instagram, Pinterest, and Facebook aren't just for socializing; they're marketplaces in their own right. Engaging content, such as tutorials, behind-the-scenes looks, or customer testimonials, can foster community and create brand ambassadors who spread the word about your products. Regular interaction with your audience strengthens relationships and builds trust.

Don't underestimate the power of email marketing either. Building an email list and crafting personalized, value-driven messages can lead to repeat business and customer loyalty. Customers who feel seen and understood are more likely to return, and email is one of the most direct ways to communicate with them.

Analytics and customer feedback should shape your long-term strategy. Leveraging data helps you understand what's working and what's not, allowing you to refine your tactics and offerings continually. Don't just focus on the numbers; pay attention to the stories they tell. Understanding customer behavior is an ongoing process that requires adaptability and a keen eye for opportunities.

Lastly, remember that e-commerce is as much about resilience as it is about strategy. Challenges and setbacks are part of the process. Staying informed about market trends and technological advancements can keep you ahead of the curve. Adaptation is key in the fast-paced world of digital commerce.

E-commerce is an ever-evolving field that demands not only creativity and strategy but also a willingness to learn and grow continually. By grasping these essentials, you're not merely building an online store; you're crafting a brand and creating a community. The e-commerce world is rich with opportunities for those willing to explore and innovate. As you apply these essentials, you step closer to building a sustainable and rewarding online business.

Setting Up an Online Store

Diving into e-commerce is like embarking on a grand adventure in the digital realm, filled with endless possibilities and potential rewards. Setting up an online store requires a mix of creativity, strategy, and a dash of entrepreneurial spirit. This journey begins with a vision—a clear understanding of what you want to sell and who your customers will be. Whether you're passionate about custom-made crafts or drawn to dropshipping, the key is to offer something that resonates with your audience.

Choosing the right e-commerce platform is crucial to your store's success. Platforms like Shopify, WooCommerce, and BigCommerce offer a range of features that cater to different needs. For those just starting out, look for a platform that balances ease of use with robust functionality. A user-friendly interface can save you countless hours, allowing you to focus on what truly matters—growing your business. Consider scalability as well. As your store expands, you'll want a platform that can grow with you, accommodating increased traffic and diversified inventory.

Once you've selected a platform, it's time to design your store. This step is where your brand comes to life. From the color scheme to the font style, every element should tell your story and align with your brand identity. The goal is not just to create something that looks good, but also to craft an experience that speaks to your customers' sensibilities. Remember, the online shopping experience should be seamless and enjoyable, prompting customers to come back for more.

Don't underestimate the power of product photos and descriptions—they can make or break a sale. Clear, high-quality images allow customers to visualize what they are purchasing, while engaging descriptions provide context and highlight key features and benefits. Think beyond just listing specifications; share stories or scenarios that help potential customers imagine their lives enhanced by your product.

The technical setup might seem daunting, but it's an essential building block. This includes domain registration, web hosting, and setting up a secure payment gateway. Customers need to trust that their personal and payment information is safe when shopping with you. SSL certification and compliance with data protection regulations are non-negotiable in today's e-commerce landscape.

Next, consider logistics: shipping and handling. Decide whether you'll manage these in-house or partner with a fulfillment service. Analyze costs, delivery times, and your own capacity for handling orders. A transparent and efficient logistics process not only enhances customer satisfaction but can also be a significant competitive advantage.

Your store policies regarding returns, refunds, and customer service need to be clear and visible. These policies should reflect your commitment to customer satisfaction and serve as a reassurance to buyers that they're making a risk-free purchase. Good customer service isn't just about handling complaints; it's about fostering a relationship that encourages loyalty and repeat business.

Pricing your products strategically can help you stand out. Understanding your market and competitors is vital here. Consider your costs, perceived value, and what customers are willing to pay. Offering bundles, discounts, or loyalty programs can be effective in driving sales, but ensure these won't undermine your brand's value.

Launching an online store is just the beginning; the real work lies in attracting customers. This is where effective marketing strategies come into play. Utilize SEO practices to improve your store's visibility on search engines. Social media marketing, email campaigns, and influencer partnerships are also valuable tools that can extend your reach and boost engagement.

Tracking and analytics dashboards are indispensable for assessing your store's performance. They offer insights into traffic patterns, conversion rates, and customer behaviors, helping you make informed decisions. Regularly analyzing this data can help identify what's working, what isn't, and where you need to pivot.

Engagement with your audience doesn't end after a purchase. Establish a feedback loop by encouraging reviews and testimonials. Positive reviews can amplify trust and credibility, while constructive criticism provides insights into areas of improvement. Listening to your customers and adapting accordingly is a hallmark of successful e-commerce ventures.

Starting an online store is like planting a seed. It requires patience, nurturing, and resilience. Challenges will arise, from managing competition to adapting to market changes, but each obstacle is an opportunity to learn and grow. The digital world offers unparalleled opportunities to scale your store beyond geographical constraints, turning your small idea into a thriving online business.

Keep your passion at the heart of your venture. This zeal will not only drive you but also resonate with your customers. As you embark on this journey, remember that every great online store started with just a single click—a dream brought to life through determination, a keen eye for opportunity, and the courage to venture into the unknown.

Effective Product Marketing

When we hear the term "product marketing," what often comes to mind is the slick, visually appealing advertisements that gracefully slide into our social media feeds. But in the world of e-commerce, effective product marketing runs much deeper than eye-catching images or catchy slogans. For aspiring entrepreneurs and side hustlers diving into e-commerce, understanding the nuances of marketing can spell the difference between a digital shelf collector and a bestseller.

Let's consider the buyer's journey. Understanding how potential customers find your product, what drives their decision to click "add to cart," and why they return—or don't—is crucial. So, what's the secret sauce? Connection. Effective product marketing hinges on establishing a genuine connection with your audience. It's about showing that what you offer solves a problem, meets a need, or enhances their life in some meaningful way.

One never-ending truth in e-commerce is the power of storytelling. A great product story can captivate and convert skeptics into loyal customers. It's not just about the product itself but about the experience. How does it align with your customer's values and aspirations? For instance, a skincare brand might not just talk about their moisturizers' ingredients but rather the confidence it gives users to face the world every morning. When marketed effectively, products don't just fill a void—they enhance stories, improve endeavors, and sometimes even alter lifestyles.

Now, let's delve into one of the key strategies of effective product marketing: differentiation. In a saturated market, standing out is imperative. This isn't simply about having a unique product but also about how you present it. Does your product come with outstanding customer service or an innovative guarantee? Or perhaps it's locally sourced, which speaks to an eco-conscious consumer base. Highlight these unique value propositions boldly and clearly.

Social proof serves as a catalyst in product marketing. In an age where consumers are bombarded with choices, reviews, testimonials, and user-generated content can lend credibility and play a significant role in the decision-making process. Encourage customers to leave feedback and display these tidbits of validation where prospects can easily find them. It not only builds trust but also enhances the perception of your product's value.

Visuals aren't just nice-to-haves; they're essential. High-quality images and engaging videos can dramatically lift the appeal of your e-commerce products. In a virtual marketplace, customers can't touch or try the product, so conveying quality through visuals becomes paramount. Make sure every photo showcases not just the product, but what owning it could feel like. Layer this with compelling product descriptions, and you've got yourself a powerful combo.

Next up is employing tailored email marketing strategies, which proves remarkably effective for nurturing leads and boosting sales. When done right, email campaigns provide a personal touch that feels exclusive and makes customers feel valued. Segment your list and tailor communications based on past interactions, recommendations, and interests. This kind of personalization goes a long way in winning over customers and maintaining loyalty.

Let's not forget the importance of aligning your marketing efforts with the right channels. It's not just about being present on every platform but nailing where your target audience predominantly resides. This way, you're not scattering efforts wide across the digital landscape, but rather focusing on where you're most likely to convert interested eyes into loyal customers. Remember, it's quality over quantity.

Pricing strategies can also significantly impact the perceived value of your product. Do your research and understand what competitors are charging, but don't be afraid to command a premium if your product warrants it. It's not just about being the cheapest option on the shelf. Luxury brands thrive not just because of the materials but because of the perceived status and exclusivity. Strategically pricing your products can create a similar dynamic.

Leveraging the power of limited-time offers and exclusive sales can create urgency and drive immediate action. Whether through countdown timers or special member-only discounts, these strategies tap into consumer psychology, compelling them to act before it's too late. Done strategically, promotions can boost short-term sales while building long-term brand love.

Finally, consider adopting a holistic approach where every touchpoint with the customer is an opportunity. Whether it's through post-purchase communication, helpful online resources, or consistent brand messages that resonate, building relationships doesn't end at the sale. Follow-up and bring customers on a continuous journey with your brand. Adopt a mindset of growth and learning, iterating upon what works and quickly shedding what doesn't.

Effective product marketing is no overnight achievement, but with dedication and a genuine desire to serve your audience, the results can be transformative. Your products can become more than commodities—they can become an integral part of your customer's lives. Keep refining and reimagining, because the art of marketing never stands still, and neither should your aspirations. Stay inspired, stay innovative, and most importantly, stay connected. That's the heart of successful product marketing in e-commerce.

Chapter 5: Affiliate Marketing Success

Transitioning from e-commerce and blogging into the world of affiliate marketing feels like a natural progression. It's akin to recommending a favorite restaurant to a friend, except now you're getting paid for it. But let me tell you, it's more than just throwing a bunch of links on a website. Achieving success in affiliate marketing requires strategy, creativity, and an understanding of your audience.

At its most basic, affiliate marketing is a performance-based model where a business rewards you—a publisher or content creator—for generating sales or traffic through your referrals. It's like being a bridge between a consumer and a business. However, it's important to understand that success doesn't come from simply promoting any product or service. The key lies in authenticity and alignment with your brand. Ask yourself: Does this product resonate with my audience? Would I use it myself? If you can't answer "yes" with confidence, it's time to rethink your strategy.

Choosing the right affiliate programs to partner with is critical. Hundreds of programs exist, ranging from large networks to individual brands offering affiliate opportunities. Research needs to be thorough. Read reviews, understand the commission structures, and most importantly, evaluate the trustworthiness of the programs. Look for programs that have a good reputation, favorable commission rates, and a product or service that you genuinely believe in. This authenticity will shine through in your promotions, building trust with your audience.

Your next step is maximizing affiliate earnings. Here's the thing—it's often not just about the volume of traffic. The quality of your targeting and your understanding of audience needs can elevate your campaigns. Embrace analytics to track which links are performing well. Don't be afraid to experiment with placement—sometimes a link in the middle of a blog post works better than a banner ad. Consistently refine your approach based on what the data tells you. Remember, affiliate marketing isn't a passive endeavor; it's an evolving art.

Diversifying your affiliate income streams can help bolster your profits. Don't rely on a single program or market to sustain your earnings. Consider partnering with multiple programs across different niches relevant to your audience. This not only reduces risk but can significantly increase your potential income. Balance is crucial; you want a variety of programs without overwhelming your content with an overload of affiliate links.

Creativity plays a pivotal role in standing out from the crowd. Content marketing is your best friend. Whether it's through engaging blog posts, immersive videos, or informative podcasts, the way you deliver affiliate links can make all the difference. Feel free to weave personal stories or experiences with products into your promotions. This personal touch creates a connection and adds a level of trust, making your recommendations feel more genuine and less like a sales pitch.

Building a community around your content can further aid your efforts. Engage with your audience, foster discussions, and encourage feedback. A strong community not only amplifies your reach but also offers insights into your audience's preferences, helping tailor your affiliate strategies even more effectively. Consider hosting webinars or live Q&A sessions where you can discuss the products you're promoting, giving real-time insights and answering questions promptly.

The path to affiliate marketing success is filled with both challenges and rewarding moments. It's a journey of continuous learning and adaptation. Stay informed about industry trends, new technologies, and evolving consumer behaviors. Leverage this knowledge to stay ahead, and always aspire to bring value with your promotions. When you align your efforts with the needs of your audience and the strengths of your platform, affiliate marketing can transform into a thriving income stream.

Embrace the journey, adapt swiftly, and infuse genuine enthusiasm into your work. With the right mindset and strategies, you're on the path to unlocking the full potential of affiliate marketing—and in turn, diversifying your income in the digital landscape. Your success lies in the passion you bring and the authenticity you maintain, turning opportunities into sustained success.

Choosing Profitable Programs

Imagine standing at the edge of a vast ocean, wading through an abundance of affiliate marketing programs, each promising a sea of opportunities. Yet, with such abundance comes the genuine challenge of discernment. How does one choose the right tide to ride towards profitability? That's what we'll dive into here, exploring strategies that help you find programs that align with your goals and ensure substantial returns on your investments of time and effort.

First and foremost, it's essential to understand your audience. Who are these people you're aiming to reach? What are their needs, desires, and pain points? The more intimately you know them, the better you can align your choice of affiliate programs with their interests. This isn't just about making a sale; it's about providing genuine value, something that resonates with them, and becomes a solution to their problems. The programs you choose should naturally fit into this narrative, enhancing their journey while supporting your own objectives.

Next, consider the reliability and reputation of the affiliate programs you're evaluating. In an industry sometimes plagued with ambiguity, aligning with reputable brands can have a substantial impact not just on your earnings, but on your credibility. Look for programs with a long-standing history, ample positive reviews, and transparent business practices. Trustworthiness is a currency in its own right, and affiliating with brands known for theirs can elevate your status in the eyes of your audience, ensuring that any engagements lead to fruitful outcomes.

Variety is the spice of life—and affiliate marketing is no different. While you might be inclined to focus on a single niche or product line, diversifying your portfolio always pays dividends. Explore programs that offer complementary products or services within your chosen field. This diversity not only cushions any potential downturns in one area but also broadens the earning opportunities across various segments.

Think of it as not packing all your eggs into one basket, and you'll see why versatility can be a game-changer.

Don't underestimate the power of commission structures while choosing profitable programs. A higher commission rate might catch your eye, but it's crucial to dig deeper. Understand how the commission is calculated. Is it a flat rate or a percentage? Are there tiered levels based on performance milestones? Knowing the fine print can help maximize your earning potential. Sometimes, a lower percentage on a high-ticket item could be more rewarding than a high percentage on a low-cost product.

Equally important is the support and resources the affiliate program offers. High-quality programs often provide their partners with a slew of resources—marketing materials, analytics, training sessions, and support channels. These resources are not just add-ons; they are investments in your success. Having a wealth of tools at your disposal can significantly streamline your marketing efforts, allowing you to focus more on driving conversions rather than developing collateral from scratch.

It's also worth considering the longevity of the program. Trends come and go, and the last thing you want is to invest your time and resources into a program that's not built to last. Look for products or services that are not only trendy but also have staying power. They should solve enduring problems or cater to perennial needs. Programs targeting niche markets, such as sustainable living or tech gadgets, can often remain profitable despite broader market shifts.

Remember, choosing profitable programs is not just about what they can do for you today but what they can do tomorrow and beyond. Establishing strong relationships with program managers can provide insights into product pipelines and upcoming changes. Being in the know can give you a competitive edge, allowing you to adjust your strategies proactively rather than reactively.

Finally, listen to your own experiences. Your performance data is an invaluable tool. Analyze what's worked in the past and what's fallen short. Understand the why behind each campaign's success or failure. This data-driven approach will help you refine your program choices and strategies, ensuring a virtuous cycle of continuous improvement and success.

In closing, choosing profitable programs is an art combined with science. It requires intuition, data evaluation, and a keen understanding of market dynamics. By carefully selecting programs that align with both your personal affinities and audience needs, your affiliate marketing ventures can not only provide an effective income stream but can also yield incredible personal growth and industry influence. The path to affiliate marketing success is nuanced, but with a strategic approach, it is undeniably rewarding.

Maximizing Affiliate Earnings

You've laid the groundwork for affiliate marketing success by choosing profitable programs. Now, let's dive into the strategies that'll maximize your earnings and bring your success to new heights. Affiliates often focus on expanding their reach while honing in on tactics that convert visitors into buyers. This balance requires a nuanced mix of creativity, diligence, and keen market insights.

First, it's crucial to understand your audience. As an aspiring entrepreneur, you can't simply broadcast a generic message and expect results. Diving deep into your niche allows you to craft content that resonates with your audience on a personal level. Personalization is not just a buzzword; it's a game-changer. Customize your approach based on demographic insights, preferences, and purchasing behaviors. The more you align your messaging with your audience's needs, the higher the likelihood they'll trust your recommendations and, eventually, make a purchase.

The next cornerstone of maximizing affiliate earnings is leveraging data to your advantage. Sure, creativity fuels compelling campaigns, but data analysis keeps the ship steady. Modern digital marketing offers a huge volume of actionable data. Whether it's through Google Analytics or the analytics tools of your chosen affiliate platform, there's a wealth of information to be tapped into. Monitor click-through rates, conversion ratios, and even the time your audience spends on pages. This data tells a story—one that helps you refine your strategies. It's not just about what products you promote, but how you promote them.

But how exactly should one promote affiliate products effectively? Diversity in promotion channels plays a significant role here. Blending different mediums not only increases visibility but also caters to various segments of your audience. Consider blogs, podcasts, videos, and social media as different stages for your performance. Sometimes it's a well-crafted blog post that does the trick, while at other times, a tutorial video might show the product in action more convincingly. A mix keeps your content dynamic and constantly engaging.

Speaking of engagement, don't underestimate the power of storytelling. Humans are wired to connect with stories. Instead of presenting a product flatly, weave it into a narrative that your audience can find relatable. Share personal experiences, or even better, share stories from others who have benefited from the product you're promoting. Make it relatable. The empathy and connection generated through storytelling can significantly enhance your audience's trust and responsiveness.

Once you've captured your audience's interest through storytelling, cultivating an ongoing relationship ensures that your influence grows stronger over time. Consider creating a newsletter to keep your audience engaged with regular insights, tips, and exclusive offers. This not only maintains engagement but also builds a sense of community. When readers see you as an authority they trust, it's easier to recommend products, and your chances of successful conversions increase.

Another robust strategy is to optimize your content for search engines. SEO remains a steadfast pillar of online marketing. By enriching your content with relevant keywords, meta tags, and descriptions, you increase the organic reach of your content. SEO might seem daunting, but starting with on-page SEO essentials and gradually diving into more advanced tactics can substantially elevate your affiliate game. The beauty of SEO is its long-term benefits; unlike paid ads, it keeps yielding results over time as your content climbs search engine rankings.

In addition to SEO, think about harnessing the power of automation. Setting up automated email sequences, chatbots, or retargeting ads can keep your affiliate campaigns running smoothly—even when you're not actively managing them. Automation frees up time to focus on strategic thinking and growth-oriented tasks, ensuring consistent engagement with minimal effort.

Loyalty programs and exclusive offers can further galvanize your audience to act decisively. If your affiliate program allows flexibility in offering discounts or bonuses, leverage this to your advantage. People love a good deal or feeling like they're part of something exclusive. It's a subtle way of driving up the urgency while making your audience feel special.

Moreover, collaboration can be a powerful ally. Engaging with other influencers or partners in your niche can introduce your content to wider audiences. This doesn't only amplify reach but enriches your offering with diverse perspectives and potential new product lines. Consider joint webinars, interviews, or guest blogging. Collaboration is synergy in action, multiplying the potential of individual efforts.

Finally, remain adaptable and open to change. The digital landscape is relentless in its dynamism, and the key to longevity is adaptability. By staying updated with market trends and emerging tools, you're always positioned with a competitive advantage. Experimenting with new strategies, keeping an ear to the ground for industry innovations, and continuous learning ensures your affiliate endeavors remain fresh and effective.

Maximizing affiliate earnings involves more than just following a set of steps—it's about adapting a mindset of growth, creativity, and continual improvement. With commitment and the right strategies, you're not just diversifying your income; you're empowering yourself to achieve financial independence in the evolving digital marketplace. Stay persistent and embrace the journey fully, continuously strive to refine your approach. Your dedication will pay off in the form of a thriving affiliate marketing venture.

Chapter 6: Creating and Selling Digital Products

In today's fast-paced digital economy, creating and selling digital products isn't just an opportunity—it's a strategic move towards financial independence. We're living in a world where geographical boundaries have become virtually irrelevant and creativity is currency. This chapter is your roadmap to harnessing that creativity into tangible, income-generating digital products. Whether it's an eBook, a software tool, or a course, the beauty of digital products lies in their scalability and accessibility. With the right strategy, your ideas can reach a global audience, creating income with virtually no limit.

The first step in this journey is identifying the right type of digital product to create. It's crucial to not only follow your passions but to also understand where market demand meets your expertise. This intersection is your sweet spot. Digital products come in various forms—think about eBooks, online courses, templates, software, even exclusive content memberships. Each product type has its unique set of advantages, so consider what best aligns with your strengths and what your potential audience craves.

One significant advantage of digital products over physical ones is the low overhead costs. There is no inventory needed, no shipping logistics to worry about. Once you've created your product, it exists in perpetuity, ready for anyone who wants to purchase it. This doesn't mean it's a walk in the park, but understanding this can motivate you to push through the initial phase of development.

Now, let's talk about execution. Creating a digital product requires a blend of creativity, research, and technical skills. It begins with an idea, but you must nourish this idea with diligent research. Find out what your potential customers are looking for. Use tools like keyword analysis and social media polls to understand their needs and pain points. This research phase is where you'll plant the seeds for a product that people are eager to buy.

In terms of production, the process varies greatly based on the type of product. An eBook, for instance, will require solid writing skills and design finesse, while software development calls for technical programming knowledge. Don't be afraid to collaborate or outsource tasks that fall outside your area of expertise. This can help you maintain a high quality and save valuable time. Remember, focus on what you do best and let others do the rest.

Setting a price for your digital product can feel daunting. Price too high, and you risk alienating potential customers; price too low, and you may devalue your work. A successful pricing strategy often lies in understanding perceived value. Research what competitors charge and think about what makes your product stand out. Consider tiered pricing or offering complimentary mini-products that add perceived value and encourage larger purchases.

With your product polished and priced, it's time to think about distribution. The beauty of the digital realm is there's no shortage of platforms to host and sell your product. From established marketplaces like Amazon and Etsy to your own website, the options are plentiful. Consider your audience's behaviors when choosing a platform—where do they spend most of their time? How do they prefer purchasing products? Use these insights to guide your distribution strategy.

Marketing plays an integral role in the success of your digital product. Without it, even the most brilliant products can go unnoticed. Create a marketing plan that leverages a mix of strategies—like social media, email marketing, or content marketing—and amplify it with paid advertising if budget permits. Building a community around your product and engaging them through meaningful content can transform customers into brand advocates.

Lastly, never underestimate the power of adaptation and feedback. The digital landscape evolves rapidly, and so should your strategies. Seek feedback, listen to your audience, and be flexible enough to pivot when necessary. This iterative approach not only helps improve your current offerings but can also spark ideas for new products.

Creating and selling digital products is an empowering journey. It grants you the creative freedom to follow your passions while potentially generating income that grows exponentially. As you dive into this digital frontier, stay driven by your vision, adapt through learning, and keep an eye on the horizon for the next exciting opportunity.

Types of Digital Products

In the expansive realm of digital entrepreneurship, the choice of what to create and sell can be both exhilarating and overwhelming. The possibilities spread out in front of you like an endless canvas. But fear not—understanding the types of digital products available can illuminate your path and guide your efforts toward crafting something both meaningful and profitable. It's about channeling the creativity within you to impact audiences across the globe while building a viable business model. Let's delve into the diverse types of digital products that can form the cornerstone of your online venture.

E-books: For many entrepreneurs, e-books represent the first foray into creating digital goods. They're accessible to produce and distribute, allowing you to share expertise, tell stories, or compile research without the logistical hassles of publishing physical books. E-books appeal to readers who crave immediate access to knowledge. Moreover, given the explosion of e-readers and smartphones, the market for e-books continues to flourish with incredible potential for scalability.

Online Courses: Knowledge is power, they say, and there has never been a better time to share yours. Online courses have surged in popularity, offering an interactive way to educate audiences while generating income. With platforms vying for attention, you can choose where and how to teach. Whether you're passionate about digital marketing, creative writing, or coding, structuring an online course can be a fulfilling and lucrative endeavor. A well-designed course can not only enlighten and inspire but also establish your credibility as an expert in your field.

Software and Apps: In a tech-driven world, creating software or apps can be exceptionally rewarding. Think about how effortlessly apps have integrated into daily life—there's a constant demand for tools that simplify, entertain, or solve problems. Whether you're keen on developing productivity software, lifestyle apps, or even engaging games, the possibilities are as exciting as they are endless. With the right approach, your software or app could become an indispensable part of people's lives.

Membership Sites: If you've got valuable, ongoing content to share, consider creating a membership site. This type of digital product leverages the power of community and recurring revenue. By offering exclusive access to content, forums, or resources for a monthly fee, you ensure a steady income stream while nurturing a dedicated audience. Membership sites thrive on delivering continuous value, so the bond you build with your members can be incredibly strong.

Digital Art and Graphics: For the creatively inclined, selling digital art and graphics can be emotionally rewarding and potentially profitable. From vector illustrations and digital paintings to stock photos and design assets like templates and fonts, this category allows artists to reach wider audiences. The need for unique, high-quality digital art is pervasive across web design, advertising, and personal projects, creating abundant opportunities to turn your creativity into cash.

Music and Audio Files: Gone are the days when artists had to rely solely on record labels to distribute their music. The digital age has democratized music production and sales, opening new avenues for musicians to sell their work directly to fans worldwide. Additionally, audio files catering to niche markets like meditation, sound effects, and podcasting have found their places in the digital economy. If sound is your passion, then this path might resonate with you.

Templates and Tools: Business owners and creatives alike are always on the lookout for tools that'll make their lives easier. Designing templates—for websites, resumes, or presentations—can serve this need while providing you with a steady income stream. Digital tools like calculators, trackers, or spreadsheets can also be packaged and sold, offering time-saving solutions to busy professionals. Consider what people need, look for areas where you can add value, and offer them a ready-made shortcut.

Printable and Digital Stationery: In a world where personalization counts, printable and digital stationery offer a charming means of expression. These can range from invitations, planners, and calendars to journal pages and business cards. With increasing numbers of people turning to digital resources to elevate their tasks and personal projects, stationery items offer both utility and creative outlet. Aesthetics play a key role, so if design is your forte, this avenue might just be your passion project.

As you embark on the journey of creating and selling digital products, remember that the key lies in understanding the value you bring to the table. Each type of product caters to a different audience and serves unique purposes. The beauty of digital products is that they allow you to tap into your personal strengths and passions. So, harness them wisely. In this ever-evolving digital landscape, the intersection of creativity, technology, and entrepreneurship can lead to opportunities only limited by your imagination.

Pricing and Distribution Strategies

Pricing your digital product isn't just a matter of picking a number and running with it. It's a strategic dance that reflects your value proposition, target market, and the landscape of the competition. When it comes to pricing, consider the psychological impact on your buyers. A well-chosen price can either invite a sense of trust and value, or inadvertently scare potential customers away. For many aspiring entrepreneurs, it starts with understanding perceived value. Your pricing strategy requires a nuanced balance between what you think your product is worth and what your customers are willing to pay.

It's crucial to analyze market trends and competitor pricing. Too low, and you risk undermining your product's value while running dangerously close to overextending yourself financially. Too high, and you might alienate a portion of your audience not ready to commit at that price. A comprehensive market analysis can offer a clearer picture of where your product stands, allowing you to position it optimally in the digital marketplace. Don't shy away from testing different price points to see what resonates best with your audience.

Tiered pricing is a strategy that allows for flexibility and appeals to a wider range of customers. By creating different packages or versions of your product, you can cater to both budget-conscious consumers and those ready to invest for premium features. Offering a basic version alongside a mid and a high-end option provides a ladder that customers can climb as they perceive more value from your offerings. This method not only maximizes profit potential but also gives your customers the choice of how they want to experience your product.

Another powerful approach is to create a sense of urgency with limited-time offers or exclusivity. Techniques such as early-bird pricing for products or setting a deadline for discount prices can spur potential customers into action. By utilizing scarcity and urgency, you're tapping into the psychological phenomenon known as FOMO—fear of missing out. This can be a compelling motivator, pushing those on the fence to commit to purchasing.

When we shift to distribution strategies, remember that the digital landscape is rich with options. Your choice of distribution channels will heavily influence your product's visibility and accessibility. Whether your products are e-books, online courses, or software applications, it's important to select the platforms that align with your audience's habits and preferences. Do they prefer downloads from your personal website, or are they more inclined to purchase through established marketplaces like Amazon or Etsy?

Direct-to-consumer sales channels offer a great degree of control and higher profit margins. Selling through your own website allows you to cultivate a brand experience that's entirely aligned with your vision. You maintain complete oversight over the customer's journey, from landing page to checkout. However, this route demands robust marketing efforts to drive traffic and encourage conversions.

Using third-party platforms might mean sharing a portion of your earnings, but they often come with a built-in audience. These platforms can be gateways to heightened visibility and established trust, both critical in the early stages of your digital product's life. This can be particularly advantageous for those without a large existing audience but looking to tap into a ready pool of potential buyers.

Email marketing remains a time-tested channel for distributing your digital product. By building and nurturing an email list, you can communicate directly with your audience, offering personalized experiences and updates. This creates an invaluable direct line to offer promotions, upsell additional products, and gather feedback. Crafting compelling email campaigns with clear calls to action can significantly enhance the effectiveness of your distribution strategy.

Social media platforms also play a part in your distribution tactics. Leveraging social commerce can provide your audience with seamless purchasing experiences right within the platforms they frequently use.

It encourages impulse buys and makes it easier for your content to be shared and distributed organically. Scaling out your distribution using social media allows you to tap into the viral potential of these platforms, harnessing their power to amplify your reach exponentially.

Promotional partnerships can further extend the reach of your distribution efforts. Networking with influencers or affiliates who resonate with your target audience can provide social proof and broaden your exposure. Strategic partnerships enable you to tap into networks you may not have direct access to, lending credibility and introducing your product to potential customers who trust these voices.

As you refine your pricing and distribution strategies, remember that flexibility and adaptation are key. Customer preferences and market conditions evolve, and so must your approach. Stay open to feedback and willing to adjust your pricing tiers or distribution channels as necessary to maintain alignment with your audience's shifting needs and expectations. By doing so, not only will you sustain a competitive edge in the ever-changing digital landscape, but you'll also reinforce the trust and loyalty of your customer base.

Ultimately, the successful sale of your digital product relies on a strategic blend of pricing intelligence and shrewd distribution choices. When these elements come together seamlessly, they unlock the potential for generating significant income while reinforcing your brand's value in the eyes of your customers. Keep in mind that the journey doesn't end after the initial sale; it's a continuum of engaging and nurturing your audience, cementing a foundation for ongoing success.

Chapter 7: Navigating the World of Freelancing

Diving into freelancing can be both exhilarating and daunting. It's a realm filled with boundless opportunities, yet there's an equal measure of uncertainty. For aspiring entrepreneurs, freelancing represents a chance to embrace flexibility and creative freedom. By understanding this dynamic landscape, you can turn potential challenges into stepping stones for success.

First, it's important to identify your niche skills. Look at what you already excel at, and think about how those skills can be transformed into freelance services. Whether it's writing, graphic design, programming, or social media management, there's a market for your unique talents. Knowing your strengths is fundamental because it enables you to offer specialized services, rather than being a jack-of-all-trades.

Building a diverse client base is the next step. While it may be tempting to latch onto the first client that comes your way, diversification is key in freelancing. Relying on a single client for all your income mirrors the risks of traditional employment. When you diversify, you not only spread your risk but also expand your network, inviting more opportunities for growth. Platforms like Upwork, Freelancer, and Fiverr can be excellent starting points, but don't limit yourself to them. Consider reaching out to businesses in your area or using LinkedIn to connect with potential clients.

Finding work in freelancing is often about *visibility*. Much like entrepreneurs need marketing strategies for their businesses, freelancers must market their services. Showcase your work through an online portfolio, leverage social media, and gather testimonials from satisfied clients. These steps contribute to building a trustworthy brand. Your reputation is your currency, so invest time in developing it.

The freelancing journey is heavily influenced by *client relationships*. Communicating effectively with your clients is crucial. Clear and transparent communication establishes trust and sets expectations straight from the beginning. Moreover, be open to feedback and willing to make adjustments. Such a collaborative approach not only ensures client satisfaction but also paves the way for repeat business and referrals.

Pricing your services correctly is another substantial consideration. Charge too little, and you may find yourself overwhelmed and underpaid. Charge too much, and you might scare off potential clients. Research industry standards, assess the complexity and time commitment of each project, and set a rate that reflects your experience and expertise. As you gain more experience, don't hesitate to adjust your fees accordingly.

Freelancing also demands a degree of **financial acumen**. Unlike traditional jobs, where taxes and benefits might be automatically accounted for, freelancers need to plan for these themselves. Setting aside a portion of your income for taxes and creating a buffer for leaner times is essential.

Finally, maintaining motivation and productivity can be a constant challenge in freelancing. Without the structure of a conventional workplace, it's easy to fall prey to procrastination. Establish a routine that mirrors a typical working day. Break down tasks into manageable chunks, set deadlines for yourself, and take breaks to avoid burnout. Balance is vital to sustaining a y freelancing career.

While freelancing comes with its set of hurdles, it also offers unparalleled freedom and the potential for substantial rewards. By understanding the nuances of this field and employing strategic planning, you can turn freelancing into not just a source of income, but a pathway to professional fulfillment.

Ultimately, freelancing isn't just a way to make money; it's an opportunity to design a lifestyle aligned with your aspirations and values. It's about creating a career on your own terms, filled with both exciting prospects and valuable lessons. So embrace this journey with open arms, and you'll find that freelancing can be as enriching personally as it is professionally.

Identifying Niche Skills

In the sprawling landscape of freelancing, carving out your place can feel daunting. Yet, one of the most powerful ways to establish yourself is by identifying and honing niche skills. These are specialized talents or abilities that might not be widely possessed but are in demand, allowing you to offer something unique to potential clients. Finding these niches isn't just about looking at what you already know but also about exploring how you can expand or pivot your existing skills to fit emerging needs.

Think of niche skills as hidden gems waiting to be uncovered—valuable not only because they're rare but because they offer precise solutions to distinct problems. When looking into freelancing, ask yourself: What am I already good at that others might not be? What interests me enough that I would invest time to become exceptional at it? By focusing on these areas, you pave a path that not only sets you apart but also maximizes your earning potential. Remember, freelancing isn't just about broad abilities; it's about specializing and dominating your chosen field.

Start with introspection. Examine your hobbies, past work experiences, or even academic achievements. Do any of these areas differentiate you from the crowd? For example, if you're a graphic designer who loves traditional art methods, consider niche markets like hand-drawn illustrations or unique digital patterns. Understanding your unique blend of skills can guide you toward markets that are specific yet underserved.

Once you've identified possible niches, test their viability. The idea is to balance between what you love and what sells. Engage with potential clients or communities that align with your prospective niches. Get active on forums, social media groups, or platforms like LinkedIn where your target clients might gather. Present your ideas and gauge their interest—would they value your skill, and more importantly, would they pay for it?

Don't be afraid to evolve. The online world is dynamic, and niche skills that are relevant today might change. Continuous learning and adaptation are part of keeping your freelancing journey thriving. Take online courses, attend workshops, or participate in webinars that strengthen and expand your skill set. Curious about programming? Dive into a coding bootcamp. Interested in marketing? A course on SEO or social media algorithms might be just what you need.

Networking can play a crucial role in identifying and developing your niche skills. By connecting with others in your desired field, you can learn from those who have already carved out their niche. These connections can offer valuable insights into current industry trends, emerging demands, and even potential opportunities you hadn't considered. Don't underestimate the power of mentorship within these networks.

Market research also comes into play in this discovery process. Spend time understanding the demand for certain skills in the freelancing market. Use tools to analyze job postings, search queries, and freelance platforms to see which skills are being requested. This data can illuminate gaps in the market that your niche skills could fill. Consider platforms like Upwork or Fiverr to see what's trending.

Remember, identifying niche skills is as much about mindset as it is about skill set. Be prepared to step outside of your comfort zone and take calculated risks. It's about positioning yourself as the "go-to" expert and continuously improving on that expertise. This strategic focus not only helps you stay relevant but builds a reputation that attracts a steady stream of clients.

As you refine your niche, consider the long-term vision. Think of how your skills can give you leverage in the future marketplace. Focus on building a personal brand that communicates your specialty clearly and effectively to potential clients. Your online persona, including profiles, portfolios, and social media presence, should all mirror your niche skills consistently.

The journey to identify your niche skills in freelancing might seem challenging, but it's also incredibly rewarding. By positioning yourself in a niche, you can demand higher pay rates, secure better projects, and work with inspiring clients. Not just that, but you also create a career path that is tailored to your interests and strengths, fostering a sense of fulfillment and professional satisfaction. Remember, the key is in the discovery, development, and dedication to your chosen niche.

Never forget that the end goal of identifying niche skills is not only to succeed financially but to create a career that resonates with who you are. You're not just working to live, but rather, you're living through your work—a pursuit that is both fulfilling and liberating. With each step you take towards honing those niche skills, you're not just making a career choice; you're defining your place in the digital world of freelancing.

Building a Diverse Client Base

Navigating the world of freelancing can feel like setting sail on uncharted waters. You're the captain, the navigator, and the crew, all rolled into one. A key part of steering your freelance ship towards success is building a diverse client base. Why is client diversification so crucial? Simply put, it provides stability and growth potential while offering a buffer against unforeseen economic tides. Imagine relying on a single client; if they suddenly bow out, your income sinks along with them. Diversity ensures you're spread across different markets and industries, cushioning you from the unexpected.

Diversifying your client base starts with identifying your unique skills and understanding the market demand for those skills. Consider what makes you stand out. Maybe you're a graphic designer with a knack for creating minimalist designs, or perhaps you're an SEO expert with a deep understanding of niche markets. Defining what skills you're passionate about and proficient in is the first step to identifying potential clients across various sectors. The next step? Research. It's about understanding where these skills are most needed and how you can provide value.

Once you've pinpointed your skills, it's time to dive into networking. Online platforms are goldmines for finding clients, and LinkedIn is a powerhouse for professional connections. But don't underestimate the power of niche platforms and forums relevant to your industry. Whether it's Behance for designers or GitHub for developers, engaging with communities where your skill is valued is key. Participate in discussions, share insights, and don't shy from showcasing your work. The more visible you are, the more likely you'll attract diverse clients.

Networking offline is just as critical. Attend industry conferences, workshops, and meetups to broaden your horizons. These events are filled with potential clients and collaborators seeking the expertise you offer. When engaging in these spaces, focus on building genuine connections rather than selling your services immediately. Show interest in others' projects, offer help, and the doors to diverse client opportunities will naturally open.

When you've got your foot in the door with potential clients, make sure to tailor your pitch. One-size-fits-all isn't a winning formula when it comes to securing diverse clients. Understand each client's unique needs and pain points, then customize your services to meet them. This tailored approach not only helps you win contracts but also paves the way to long-term relationships. It's these relationships that become the bedrock of a stable freelancing career.

But even with a strong pitch, not every potential client will bite. Rejection is part of the game, and handling it with grace is vital. Use it as a learning point; ask for feedback, refine your pitches, and stay persistent. The more you refine your approach, the better you'll become at converting leads into clients. Remember, every interaction is a stepping stone towards building a robust and diverse client base.

Managing a diverse client base can be a balancing act, but it's crucial for long-term success. Effective client management entails clear communication, setting expectations, and consistently delivering on your promises. Tools and applications like Trello and Asana can help you stay organized, ensuring you meet deadlines and maintain high-quality standards. Happy clients are more likely to refer you to others, further expanding your diverse network.

Feedback is your compass in this journey. Encourage your clients to give honest reviews of your work. Not only does this help you improve, but it also builds your credibility and attracts future clients. Share testimonials on your online profiles and websites to demonstrate your reliability and capability. A proven track record of satisfied clients speaks volumes and draws in diverse clientele like a magnet.

Finally, embrace the unpredictability that comes with freelancing. The markets change, industries evolve, and today's trending skills may not be in demand tomorrow. Continuously updating your skill set and adapting to new trends ensures you remain relevant. Consider taking online courses or attending workshops to expand your know-how. The more versatile you become, the more appealing you are to a wider range of clients across different industries.

In conclusion, building a diverse client base is about understanding your strengths, networking effectively, offering tailored solutions, and managing relationships with finesse. It's a continual process of learning and adapting, ensuring that your freelancing career remains afloat and thriving. By fostering a varied portfolio of clients, not only do you secure your financial footing, but you also open doors to unexpected opportunities and growth in your freelancing voyage.

Chapter 8: Investing in Online Real Estate

If you're exploring opportunities to diversify your income streams, investing in online real estate might just be your next strategic move. In today's digital age, owning virtual properties can be as lucrative as physical real estate investments, yet often requires less capital and infrastructure. This chapter will guide you through understanding the digital property landscape and how you can capitalize on it.

Online real estate refers to digital properties like domain names and websites. Buying, improving, and selling them can create substantial financial returns. It isn't unlike flipping houses, but instead, you're working with virtual spaces. The market for domain names alone has grown exponentially, with some high-profile domain flips making headlines by selling in the millions. Of course, these are rare cases, but the potential for profit is undeniable.

Let's first dive into the concept of domain flipping. Domains are much like the addresses of the internet. A good domain name is short, memorable, and can greatly enhance a brand's value online. The process typically involves purchasing domain names at a low cost and selling them for a higher price. While it sounds simple, profitable domain flipping requires skill in predicting trends and understanding market demand.

The next avenue is website flipping. This involves buying an undervalued or underperforming website, enhancing its content and functionality, and then selling it for a profit. With the right experience and research, a savvy entrepreneur can turn a little-known site into a sought-after digital property. Website flipping is more hands-on compared to domain flipping, often requiring you to optimize SEO, enhance the user experience, and improve monetization strategies.

An essential step before diving into online real estate investment is conducting a thorough evaluation. You need to assess the current market value of both domains and websites. Tools such as Estibot for domain appraisal and Flippa for website metrics provide insights into valuation. Investing time in learning how to conduct due diligence is crucial; you don't want to commit funds to a property that lacks future profit potential.

Understanding market dynamics is key to identifying profitable investments. Trends in buyer behavior, emerging technologies, and even global events can influence the value of digital properties. Staying informed through industry blogs, forums, and news can give you an edge. Networking with other investors also provides access to shared insights and potential investment opportunities.

Deciding on your investment strategy is just as important. You may choose to focus exclusively on domain names, taking advantage of your knack for trend forecasting. Or, perhaps website flipping suits you better, particularly if you have skills in web development or marketing. Whichever path you opt for, consistency and continuous learning are necessary to stay competitive in the ever-changing online terrain.

Moreover, patience is often underestimated in this industry. Unlike physical real estate, digital properties can fluctuate in value with little warning. Holding onto a domain or website until market conditions are favorable can maximize returns. On the flipside, being proactive about enhancements and ongoing management of your online assets can increase their value over time.

While initial investments can vary, the barriers to entry are relatively lower than traditional real estate. Fees for acquiring domain names start small, although premium domains demand higher budgets. Similarly, website costs can range from a few hundred to several thousand dollars depending on their current performance and potential. It's essential to plan your budget strategically, ensuring you have the means to invest in improvements for your purchases.

To sum it up, investing in online real estate is an exciting opportunity with considerable potential. Whether you're flipping domains or revamping websites, the landscape is ripe with possibilities for growth. As you consider this path, remember that success hinges on the synergy of strategic foresight, calculated risk-taking, and persistent effort. You've learned to harness the digital realm's potential; now, it's time to build your digital empire.

Understanding Domain and Website Flipping

Investing in online real estate is more than just a buzzword; it's a strategic venture that can open doors to lucrative returns. Think of the digital world as a vast landscape filled with potential, where domains and websites serve as prime parcels of virtual land. Understanding domain and website flipping isn't just about buying and selling; it's about recognizing the hidden value and potential within the online marketplace, similar to seeing future possibilities in raw, undeveloped land.

Just like in traditional real estate, the key to success in domain and website flipping is a keen eye for value. A successful flip can be achieved by purchasing undervalued domains or websites, improving them, and selling them at a profit. The process demands not just technical know-how but also market awareness and a touch of creativity. Whether you're an aspiring entrepreneur or a freelancer seeking new income streams, mastering this art can offer you both financial rewards and the satisfaction of building something from the ground up.

A domain is essentially your web address, the virtual "lot" where you can build an online presence. The value of a domain is determined by its memorability, relevance, and search engine potential. Over time, trends evolve, and a domain that might have seemed irrelevant a few years ago could suddenly become in high demand. The beauty of domain flipping lies in anticipating these shifts, investing early, and positioning yourself to sell when the time is right.

Website flipping, on the other hand, involves acquiring an already developed site, improving its content, design, or monetization strategies, and then selling it for a profit. The process can be likened to house flipping—with the right touch and understanding, a fixer-upper can transform into prime web real estate. Successful flippers not only understand technical enhancements but also content optimization, user engagement strategies, and effective monetization techniques.

For those new to this field, the journey begins with learning the market. Immersing yourself in domain and website marketplaces is crucial. Platforms like Flippa and Sedo are vibrant marketplaces where you'll witness firsthand the price fluctuations and trends. As with any investment, research is your best ally. Learn about domain name trends, understand the factors that contribute to a website's recurring income, and familiarize yourself with SEO strategies that can boost a site's visibility.

When diving into domain flipping, one strategy is to focus on niche markets. Domains that are tied to emerging industries or shifts in consumer behavior can yield impressive returns. Imagine it as spotting the right neighborhood just before it becomes trendy. Often, niche domains face less competition, allowing for more leeway in setting attractive prices during resale. However, the challenge with niche markets is the breadth of knowledge required to accurately predict profitability trends.

Website flipping requires a more hands-on approach. Once a website is acquired, enhancing its value becomes the central focus. This can involve anything from SEO improvements and user interface redesigns to more engaging content and diversified revenue streams. Imagine acquiring a website dedicated to travel blogging. By infusing it with original, high-quality content, optimized visuals, and robust affiliate links, the site becomes more appealing and valuable to potential buyers.

Website traffic is another pivotal component in determining a website's value. A site with consistent traffic patterns indicates established readership and stable advertising revenue. Growing traffic can be achieved through various means like content upgrades, better SEO techniques, or strategic partnerships. Leveraging social media to direct new visitors or guest posting on related sites can also significantly increase a site's visibility.

Mitigating risks is an essential part of domain and website flipping. Not every investment will yield a high-return, and the market is rife with volatility. Due diligence is not just recommended; it's mandatory. Evaluating potential purchases involves examining ownership history, traffic analytics, income reports, and understanding the niche you're entering. Risk management ensures that your investments are informed, deterring hasty decisions that could result in loss.

The final element in flipping is the sale process. Unlike traditional sales, digital marketplaces operate swiftly. Auctions can rise rapidly, and decisions must be prompt and informed. During the sale, transparency and communication are your best assets. It's crucial to present clear data on traffic, income, and potential growth opportunities, maintaining credibility and attracting serious buyers.

For those willing to put in the effort to learn and adapt, domain and website flipping isn't just an entry into online real estate but an avenue for creativity and entrepreneurial growth. In this venture, you're not only investing in web assets but also investing in yourself. Your ability to see potential and act decisively is your most significant asset. And remember, in the digital realm, there are always new horizons to explore.

Evaluating Profitable Investments

Navigating the waters of online real estate can feel a bit like playing a strategic game of chess. You've got to think several steps ahead and understand that every move impacts your next one. Aspiring digital investors need to distinguish between what's merely trendy and what's grounded in reliable returns. But fear not, for anyone willing to learn the ropes, there's potential for substantial rewards. Let's dive into how you can evaluate online real estate investments to build a profitable and sustaining digital portfolio.

Before placing your bets, understanding the kind of digital property you're dealing with is essential. Whether it's a domain name or a fully operational website, each asset type brings its unique set of considerations. Domains with generic names or those tied to evergreen niches tend to hold more value. However, acquiring a promising domain or website is only the beginning. Like physical properties, these assets require ongoing market evaluation and maintenance to realize their full potential.

Think of domain and website flipping as digital renovation projects. Sometimes you find a gem that's undervalued, ready for a little polish to glow. Often, it means acquiring a site that's got solid traffic but could use a makeover in terms of content, SEO, or user experience. Current trends in digital consumption—like mobile usability and fast page load times—dictate what's considered a valuable renovation. You're essentially adding value to the property, boosting its market appeal.

But how can you determine the potential profitability of a digital investment? The answer lies in a mix of data-driven analysis and intuition honed by experience. Start by scrutinizing current traffic statistics and revenue streams. Are visitors primarily coming from organic search, or are they being driven by temporary paid ads? A heavy reliance on paid traffic might indicate unsustainability.

In parallel, it's crucial to assess the website's niche. How stable or volatile is it? An investment in a niche susceptible to rapid decline isn't typically advised. Instead, aim for verticals that show upward trends in market research and consumer interest. Industries related to health, finance, and evergreen hobbies like gardening or DIY often provide stable grounds.

Once you've identified a potential investment, it's time to dive into due diligence. This involves checking everything from the seller's history in domain transactions to analyzing backlinks to ensure they're high-quality and spam-free. A thorough check of the site's SEO performance, such as keyword rankings and potential penalties, can spell the difference between success and a learning hard-lesson.

Don't neglect the technical side. A website running on outdated platforms or suffering from security vulnerabilities not only loses value but also demands time and resources for repairs. Similarly, ensure that any third-party components or plugins are up-to-date and supported; an investment in an archaic or unsupported system could quickly become a costly endeavor.

Imagine buying a car: you wouldn't close the deal without checking under the hood, right? The digital space is similar, requiring a technical audit to catch hidden flaws. It's an opportunity to mitigate risk by uncovering any lurking technical debt before you seal the deal. And trust in relationships is gold in this realm, much like in any business, so cultivate connections with reputable brokers and domain experts—they're your allies in identifying potential red flags.

Let's not forget the selling bit. Capitalizing on your investment involves strategic timing and positioning. Effective marketing, whether it's leveraging social proof or aligning with the latest trends in the niche, can significantly impact the sale price. Think through the lens of the buyer: What improvements could make this property irresistibly attractive? A comprehensive package of SEO enhancements, strong content, and appealing design could justify a premium price point.

Developing a reliable strategy for exit opportunities is equally important. You need to be aware of the best platforms for selling your digital properties, understand their fee structures, and have a clear picture of their buyer demographics. Flippa, Empire Flippers, and private sales channels each offer distinct advantages depending on your asset type.

In summing up, evaluating profitable investments in online real estate is about balancing tangible data with strategic foresight. It's not just about current performance but potential growth and resilience. Hold on to patience, as holding out for the right buyer or moment can be the key to unlocking substantial gains. This isn't a journey you take alone; learning and leveraging insights from those who've walked the path can help steer clear of pitfalls and celebrate the victories.

The digital landscape waits for those ready to claim their piece of online real estate with wisdom and perseverance. Not just a dream, this is an achievable reality for those who step up with educated daring, strategic planning, and above all, with a determined vision for what their investment journey will yield.

Chapter 9: Leveraging Social Media for Income

In today's digital world, if you're not utilizing social media to bolster your income, you're missing out on a goldmine of opportunity. The possibilities are virtually endless when it comes to tapping into these platforms to generate income streams. Whether you're starting from scratch or looking to boost existing ventures, understanding how to harness social media is vital in this ever-evolving landscape.

First things first: let's talk about the sheer reach of social media. Platforms like Instagram, TikTok, Twitter, and Pinterest boast billions of users combined. This means a ridiculously wide audience that's just waiting to be captivated by what you have to offer. And remember, success here isn't about trying to be everything to everyone—it's about finding your niche, your voice, and the right platform that aligns with your goals and brand.

Once you've identified your target platform, the key to turning social media into a revenue-generating machine lies in engaging content. You've got to think of social media not just as a marketing tool but as a storytelling platform. Whether you're showcasing products, sharing behind-the-scenes glimpses of your journey, or simply injecting some humor into the day, authenticity is imperative. It builds trust and an authentic connection with your audience, which is the foundation for any successful income stream.

Now, let's explore some ways you can monetize these platforms effectively. One common method is through partnerships and collaborations. By becoming an influencer or a respected voice in your niche, you can attract partnerships with brands that align with your values. This can lead to paid promotions, content creation deals, and affiliate marketing opportunities—all of which can become lucrative if managed wisely.

Another popular and straightforward way to monetize social media is by selling your own products or services directly to your audience. Social media gives you a platform to showcase what you offer without the overhead of a physical storefront. Tools like Facebook Shops and Instagram Shopping make it easier than ever to turn casual scrolls into purchases. Remember to focus on the customer experience and ensure that your purchasing process is smooth and user-friendly.

Building and engaging your audience is an ongoing process. Interacting with your followers, responding to comments, and acknowledging user-generated content are just a few ways to foster community. When your audience feels heard and valued, they are more likely to remain loyal to your brand, share your content, and bring in new customers.

It's also crucial not to underestimate the power of analytics. Social media platforms offer robust analytical tools that provide insights into your audience's behavior, preferences, and engagement patterns. This data is gold. Use it to refine your content strategy, optimize posting times, and even discover new demographics to target.

However, with great opportunity comes even greater competition. It's important to stay adaptable and innovative. Trends on social media shift rapidly, and what worked yesterday might not work tomorrow. Stay informed about the latest features and updates on your platform of choice, and don't be afraid to experiment with new formats and content types.

Success on social media also demands consistency and patience. It's not just about virality; it's about building lasting relationships. Set realistic goals, track your progress, and celebrate small milestones along the way. Remember, each post is a stepping stone towards building a sustainable online income.

Consider investing in paid social advertising if you have the budget for it. Ads can dramatically increase your reach and conversion rates when done correctly. Just make sure your ad content is as authentic and compelling as your organic content. Misaligned messaging can lead to lost trust and credibility.

In conclusion, making money through social media is more accessible than ever, but it requires strategic thinking, consistent effort, and a genuine connection with your audience. Dive into the world of social media with an open mind and a willingness to learn. Over time, with dedication and creativity, you can turn these platforms into powerful tools for generating income.

As you continue to explore the digital landscape, remember that the strategies you choose should align with your overall business goals and personal values. Social media is an incredible tool, and when used effectively, it has the potential to transform not just your business but also your life. So, harness its power, stay true to yourself, and watch as new opportunities unfold.

Monetizing Social Media Platforms

Social media is more than just a medium for connecting with friends and sharing personal stories; it's an untapped goldmine for generating income. As aspiring entrepreneurs, freelancers, and web-based innovators, you're in prime position to leverage these platforms to bolster your financial success. But how do you transform social media from a time-consuming hobby into a steady revenue stream? By strategically establishing your presence and offering value that resonates with your audience.

The first step in monetizing social media is choosing the right platform. Not all social media sites are created equal, and each has unique strengths. Consider where your target audience spends most of their time. Are they generating and consuming content on Instagram with its visually driven interface, or are they more likely to be networking on LinkedIn? For those aiming to attract a younger demographic, TikTok may offer unparalleled engagement potential. Identifying the right platform is crucial as it lays the foundation for the types of content you'll create.

Once you've selected your platform, the importance of authentic engagement cannot be overstated. Social media thrives on genuine interaction. It's not just about broadcasting your message but about building a community. Engage directly with your audience through comments, polls, and live sessions, encouraging conversations that generate interest and loyalty. This nurtured relationship translates into increased trust, which is crucial when the time comes to introduce monetization strategies.

One popular method of monetizing social media is through sponsored content. Brands are always on the lookout for authentic influencers who can share their products with a captive audience. This strategy works best when you're selective about the partnerships you choose. Endorsing products that genuinely align with your personal brand or lifestyle will reinforce your credibility and ensure that your audience remains engaged rather than feeling like they're simply being sold to. High-quality content that feels like a natural part of your feed is key here.

In addition to sponsored content, affiliate marketing is another viable option. By promoting products and services through special links, you earn a commission on every sale that originates from your referral. It's essential, however, to only promote products you truly believe in, as authenticity remains a potent driver of social media success. Transparency in affiliate marketing goes a long way in maintaining your followers' trust; always disclose these relationships clearly to your audience.

For content creators, platforms like YouTube offer monetization through advertising revenue. This requires meeting certain criteria, such as a minimum number of followers and watched hours, but once unlocked, it can become a consistent income stream. Ads in the middle of popular videos or before viral content can generate revenue without you needing to handle any transactions directly. Again, the key is to build a strong subscriber base first, focusing on creating content that viewers find value in watching.

Leveraging crowdfunding and Patreon is yet another path. This model is well-suited to creators who offer unique value and who can foster a loyal fanbase willing to pay for exclusive content. This strategy can include everything from behind-the-scenes looks at the creation process to specialized tools and advice relevant to your followers. It's a direct way to earn money from your content and gives your audience a sense of participation in your creative journey.

Let's not overlook the power of social commerce. Instagram and Facebook have turned into viable shopping platforms where businesses can display products directly to consumers. By tagging products in posts and utilizing shoppable stories, you create a seamless path for your followers to purchase directly through social media channels. This strategy not only boosts sales but also enhances the user experience by limiting the steps between seeing a product and buying it.

For those with a flair for exclusive content, setting up a subscription model on platforms like Instagram or Twitter's Super Follows lets your most dedicated fans support you in exchange for special insights or personalized interaction. This ensures a regular stream of income while reinforcing the bond between you and your audience.

Monetizing social media is also about recognizing ongoing trends and adapting swiftly. The digital landscape is constantly evolving, meaning new opportunities arise frequently. For instance, live streaming features across various platforms present unique monetization options through virtual gifts and tips, which fans can send during a broadcast. Adapting popular trends, like shareable challenges or themed content, also provides fresh engagement and opportunities for partnerships or sponsorships.

While maximizing social media revenue potential, it's important to strike a balance between monetization and value delivery. Oversaturating your feed with ads or promotional content can dilute brand authenticity and alienate your audience. Ensure that monetization efforts are woven into valuable content, keeping your primary focus on what drew your audience in initially. Quality remains the cornerstone of any successful social media strategy.

Finally, diversifying income streams on social media mitigates risk. By developing multiple channels of revenue, whether through ads, partnerships, direct selling, or unique content, you create a more stable digital venture that can withstand market shifts or platform changes. This multifaceted approach ensures sustainability while exploring new opportunities for growth.

Ultimately, social media offers boundless potential for income generation. By focusing on building a genuine connection with your audience, strategically selecting partnerships, and remaining agile in the face of change, you can turn your social media efforts into a lucrative endeavor that fuels your entrepreneurial journey.

Building and Engaging Your Audience

Jumping into the world of social media is like joining a never-ending conversation. But to truly leverage these platforms for income, it's essential to not only understand the mechanics of how they operate but also the dynamics of building an audience that's genuinely engaged. The community you cultivate online is more than just numbers — it's about creating real connections that translate into value, both for them and for you. Let's dive into how you can do this efficiently and meaningfully.

The first step in building an audience is knowing who they are. It's not enough to simply want followers; you need to understand what draws them in. Who are they, really? What are their interests, needs, and problems? Creating a detailed avatar of your ideal audience member will guide your content creation and help you stay focused on delivering value. Knowing your audience deeply is not just beneficial — it's crucial for meaningful engagement.

Authenticity is a buzzword that's thrown around a lot but holds substantial truth. People are drawn to real, relatable personalities, not just polished brands. Share your story, your struggles, and your successes. Be vulnerable and open about your journey as it relates to your niche. This doesn't mean airing all your dirty laundry; rather, it's about showing the human side of your brand or business. The personal connection fosters trust and loyalty, which are essential components of a thriving online community.

Social media is truly social. Engage with your audience as you would with a friend who visits you for coffee. Ask questions, reply to comments, and take feedback constructively. Your audience wants to be heard and acknowledged. Polls, Q&As, and other interactive features available on platforms like Instagram, Facebook, and Twitter should be used to their full potential. Not only does this provide you with valuable insights about your audience, but it also makes your audience feel valued and appreciated.

Content is king, but context is queen. While creating high-quality content is essential, understanding the context in which your audience consumes this content is equally important. The format, timing, and platform are all variables that can significantly impact engagement. For example, bite-sized content might work well on TikTok or Instagram Reels but may not have the same effect on LinkedIn or YouTube, where long-form content often performs better.

Don't underestimate the power of storytelling. It's an age-old art that remains effective in the digital age. Craft stories that resonate with your audience — whether they're personal anecdotes, case studies, or hypothetical scenarios that illustrate a point. Stories stick; they evoke emotions and make information memorable and shareable. As your audience begins to see themselves in your stories, your engagement with them naturally deepens.

Consistency breeds familiarity and trust. Establish a content schedule that your audience can rely on. This doesn't mean you have to post daily, but it does mean you need to have a predictable pattern. Whether it's a weekly video, a daily tip, or a monthly deep dive, consistency helps your audience know when to anticipate your content and subsequently make you a part of their routine.

Leverage collaborations and partnerships to expand your reach. Collaborating with influencers or other brands that share your values and have a similar audience can introduce you to potential followers who might have never discovered you otherwise. It's a win-win situation where both parties can benefit from each other's audience and credibility.

Integrating user-generated content can also boost your credibility and engender more robust engagement. Encourage your followers to share their experiences, testimonials, or creative uses of your product or service. This not only enriches your content feed but also empowers your audience, giving them a stake in your brand narrative.

Analytics are your best friend in this journey. Utilize the analytics tools available on your social platforms to understand what's working and what's not. It's a goldmine of data that can inform your future strategies, helping you refine and optimize your efforts. Pay attention to metrics such as engagement rates, reach, demographics, and the types of content that receive the most interaction. Remember, data is not just numbers; it's the story of your audience told through the language of clicks and views.

Finally, remember that the digital landscape is ever-evolving. What works today might not be effective tomorrow. Stay informed about platform updates, emerging trends, and changing algorithms. Keeping your ear to the ground ensures you can pivot and adapt quickly when necessary. But amidst all this, don't lose sight of your core goal: building meaningful connections. In the end, it's the human touch that will set you apart in a crowded digital world.

Building and engaging your audience is an ongoing journey, one that evolves as you and your brand grow. It's not just about followers or likes — it's about creating a supportive community, providing tangible value, and forging connections that last. With a strategic approach, a genuine desire to serve, and a keen eye on both data and industry trends, you'll not only build an audience but also ensure they are engaged and invested in your online journey for the long haul.

Chapter 10: Unlocking the Potential of Online Courses

There's a unique power in online courses that's reshaping how individuals learn and earn. Unlike traditional education systems, online courses offer a flexibility that caters to diverse lifestyles, and this adaptability opens doors for aspiring entrepreneurs and freelancers. If you have the knowledge or skills others want and need, there's an opportunity to transform those into a fulfilling source of income. This chapter focuses on how you can tap into that potential and create a sustainable income stream through online courses.

Understanding your niche is crucial. Before diving into course creation, you should be clear on what you're truly passionate about and what you excel in. This authentic enthusiasm translates into better content and more engaging experiences for learners. Start by asking yourself: What unique skills or insights do I possess? You might find that your hobbies, professional experiences, or even personal challenges could transform into valuable lessons. Once you identify your niche, you can tailor your course to meet specific needs in the market.

Creating engaging content is at the heart of any successful online course. People are drawn to courses that promise not only information but also transformation. Your goal is to guide your students from point A to point B in a way that's both interactive and enriching. Use a combination of videos, quizzes, and practical assignments to cater to different learning styles. A well-structured course that progresses logically keeps learners motivated and ensures they derive real value.

The internet is crowded with information, making it essential to differentiate your course. Tell a story that resonates with your audience. Relate your own experiences and challenges to help them connect on a personal level. This empathetic approach can transform your lessons from mere information to impactful knowledge. By integrating real-world examples and case studies, you offer clarity and context that helps learners effectively apply what they've learned.

Marketing your course requires creativity and strategy. Start by defining your target audience — understand their pain points, goals, and the platforms they frequent. Whether it's creating a community on social media or leveraging email newsletters, the key is connecting with your potential students where they are most active. Use a mix of organic tactics like blog posts and podcasts, and consider investing in targeted ads to capture a wider audience.

Your pricing strategy can make or break your success. Price your course too low, and it might be perceived as lacking value. Conversely, setting a high price without establishing the course's worth could deter potential buyers. Consider launching with a special offer or introductory price to attract initial interest and build momentum. This approach allows early adopters to provide testimonials and generate positive word-of-mouth, enhancing credibility as you move forward.

Every educator faces the challenge of student retention. Keep your students engaged by fostering an inclusive community. Encourage interactions through discussion forums or live Q&A sessions, which can create a sense of belonging and motivate learners to complete the course. Remember, a strong community doesn't just enhance the learning experience — it also serves as a powerful marketing tool, as satisfied students often become your best promoters.

Feedback is invaluable. Seek regular input from your students to continually refine and improve your offerings. Maybe certain sections of your course could be expanded, or perhaps the pacing needs adjustment. Embrace constructive criticism as a tool for growth. Over time, your course will evolve to better meet the needs of your audience, solidifying your reputation as a trusted and dynamic instructor.

Finally, technology is your ally in this endeavor. Make sure you select the right platform to host your course, considering factors like ease of use, scalability, and built-in marketing tools. Many platforms also offer analytics that provide insight into how students interact with your course, allowing you to make informed decisions about future improvements and adjustments.

Online courses are more than just a way to share knowledge; they represent a meaningful stream of income that can grow and evolve with you. They allow you to reach a global audience, breaking geographical barriers that previously limited educational opportunities. For entrepreneurs and freelancers aiming to diversify their income streams, courses offer not just flexibility, but also a chance to make a lasting impact.

In the rapidly evolving digital landscape, lifelong learning is no longer optional, but a necessity. By creating and marketing an effective online course, you're not only contributing to this cultural shift but also securing a spot for yourself in the future of education and entrepreneurship.

Designing Engaging Course Content

Creating engaging course content is like crafting a masterpiece that captivates and educates your audience simultaneously. This is the heart of any online course, and it's what sets successful courses apart from the rest. A well-crafted course not only conveys information but also inspires learners, fueling their curiosity and driving their passion for the subject matter. As you dive into designing your course, remember that you're not just imparting knowledge; you're igniting a desire to learn more.

Begin by putting yourself in the shoes of your learners. Consider their needs, challenges, and aspirations. What are they hoping to gain from your course? Understanding this will guide your content creation process, ensuring that what you offer is relevant and valuable. The goal is to build a bridge between what your learners know and where they aspire to be, using your course as the key to unlock that journey.

Next, structure your content thoughtfully. Just like a story needs a beginning, middle, and end, your course should have a clear roadmap that guides learners effortlessly from one concept to the next. Start with foundational concepts, slowly building in complexity as the course progresses. Each section should naturally flow into the next, creating a cohesive learning experience that feels intuitive rather than overwhelming.

Variety is not just the spice of life; it's the essence of engaging course content. Use a mix of instructional methods to cater to different learning styles—video lectures, quizzes, interactive exercises, and downloadable resources can all play a part. Videos can visually demonstrate concepts that are hard to convey through text alone, while quizzes provide instant feedback and reinforce learning. Interactive elements like case studies and simulations encourage learners to apply what they've learned in real-world scenarios, deepening their understanding.

Storytelling is a powerful tool you shouldn't overlook. People are naturally drawn to stories, so infuse your course with anecdotes and real-life examples that illustrate key points. These narratives create a connection and make the content more relatable. When learners see how the material applies to real-life situations, they're more likely to engage with it and retain the information.

Equally important is the tone you take in your content. It should be conversational yet authoritative, reflecting your mastery of the subject while making learners feel comfortable and inspired. Think of your course as a personal dialogue with your learners, not a formal lecture. This conversational tone keeps learners engaged and fosters a sense of community, which can be enhanced through interactive elements like discussion forums and Q&A sessions.

Feedback is essential in designing engaging course content. Create opportunities for learners to provide input at various stages of the course. Early feedback helps you refine the course in real-time, adjusting any areas that might not be resonating as you anticipated. It also demonstrates to learners that their experience is important to you, which can heighten their engagement and commitment to completing the course.

In addition, be mindful of accessibility. Make sure your course is accessible to all learners, including those with disabilities. Provide transcripts for videos, use clear and legible fonts, and ensure that any interactive elements are navigable using a keyboard. Accessibility is not just about compliance; it's about equity and creating an inclusive learning environment that welcomes everyone.

Don't forget to incorporate assessments that challenge and motivate your learners. Beyond quizzes, consider assignments that require learners to apply their knowledge creatively. Projects, peer reviews, and reflective journals can help students synthesize information in meaningful ways while giving you valuable insight into their progress and understanding.

Finally, keep your content up-to-date. The digital landscape is ever-changing, and so should your course. Regularly review and revise your material to ensure it reflects the latest trends, research, and tools in your field. Let your learners know of any updates, demonstrating your commitment to providing them with a cutting-edge learning experience.

By focusing on these strategies, your course won't just impart knowledge; it'll transform how learners perceive and engage with the subject matter. Engaging content is the cornerstone of unlocking the potential of your online course, setting the stage for its success and the success of your learners.

Marketing Your Online Course

You've crafted an online course that you believe in wholeheartedly. It's loaded with valuable insights, and you're eager for the world to see it. However, without effective marketing, even the most exceptional courses can linger in the shadows of the digital marketplace. Let's explore the strategies that can propel your course into the spotlight, connecting you with eager learners and fostering a thriving community.

First off, it's crucial to know your audience inside out. Understanding who will benefit from your course actually informs how you market it. Are they professionals looking to upskill, or perhaps hobbyists searching for a new passion project? Your promotional strategy needs to cater directly to these people, targeting the platforms they frequent and speaking the language they use. By honing in on your ideal audience, you can tailor messages that resonate deeply and inspire action.

Finding the right platforms for promotion is the next step. Consider leveraging social media channels, where the potential for viral content and brand growth is immense. But don't spread yourself thin; focus on two or three platforms where your audience is most active. Create compelling content that not only showcases the value of your course but also aligns with the interests and values of your target demographic.

Email marketing remains an incredibly effective tool for promotion. Building an email list allows you to nurture leads through personalized communication. Offer free content like webinars or eBooks that touch on the topics of your course as incentives for sign-ups. This approach not only builds trust but establishes you as an authority in your field. When it's time to introduce your course, your subscribers are already primed and interested, significantly increasing conversion rates.

Don't overlook the power of partnerships. Collaborating with influencers or other educators in your niche can broaden your reach exponentially. Guest blogging, podcast interviews, and joint webinars introduce your course to new audiences who are already interested in similar topics. These kinds of partnerships can bring invaluable social proof and credibility—essential in gaining the trust of potential students.

Crafting a compelling landing page is vital as it acts as the gateway to your course. Every element on this page—from the copy to the visuals—should communicate the transformation your course promises. Use customer testimonials and success stories to reinforce the benefits. Include a clear call-to-action that makes it easy for visitors to enroll. Remember, less is often more; a cluttered page can distract from the core message.

Price your course strategically by considering your target market, the competition, and the perceived value of your content. Experimenting with different pricing models, such as one-time payments versus subscription models, can help you optimize profitability while catering to diverse financial preferences. Don't shy away from offering limited-time discounts or bundling courses together, as these tactics can drive urgency and encourage immediate action.

Analyze and refine your marketing efforts continuously. Use analytic tools to track where your traffic is coming from and which strategies are yielding the best results. The digital landscape is dynamic, and what works today might change tomorrow. Be ready to pivot and adapt, continually iterating on your approach to align with the evolving behaviors of your audience.

Building a community around your course can significantly boost your marketing efforts. Foster engagement through active communication channels like forums or social media groups where students can connect and share their experiences. When learners feel part of a community, they're more likely to become advocates, sharing your course with their networks and creating organic growth through word-of-mouth.

Finally, don't underestimate the value of feedback. Encourage students to provide insights about their learning experience; this not only enhances your course but also informs your marketing strategies. Testimonials and reviews can be powerful tools in building trust with prospective students. Display these prominently in your marketing materials and updates.

With these strategies, you can light the path to success, making your course a beacon for those seeking knowledge in your expertise. The key is to be persistent, adaptable, and authentic in your marketing efforts. As you engage with your market and refine your approach, not only will your course reach the right audiences, but you'll also establish a meaningful and enduring presence in the digital education landscape. Your journey doesn't end with launching a course; it evolves through the relationships you build and the value you consistently deliver.

Chapter 11: Exploring Passive Income Opportunities

In the bustling world of online business, passive income remains a compelling idea for aspiring entrepreneurs. Imagine earning money even while you sleep—it's not a distant dream but a practical reality for those who approach it methodically. The allure of passive income lies in its promise of financial freedom with minimal active involvement over time. Contrary to popular belief, establishing these streams requires effort, but the long-term rewards can significantly outweigh the initial setup.

Consider the shift from trading time for money to letting your assets work for you. This transformation begins with a mindset change. Instead of thinking about how to earn more per hour, consider the systems you can create to generate income with little direct effort. It's about building a structure that continues to operate efficiently, allowing you to step back while the engine hums along. Various digital avenues, such as royalties from ebooks, affiliate marketing, or automated online stores, offer exciting opportunities for diversification.

Automation plays a vital role in passive income strategies. The digital landscape provides tools and technologies to automate tasks that traditionally required human oversight. By leveraging these tools, entrepreneurs can streamline processes and maximize efficiency. For instance, email marketing platforms can nurture potential leads, while e-commerce platforms can handle sales, inventory, and even customer support autonomously. Automation isn't just about convenience—it's about scaling your capability to earn continuously without the constant need for active participation.

Take affiliate marketing, for example. Bundled with the right strategy, it can be a steady source of income. By strategically placing affiliate links within content such as blogs or social media, you can earn commissions without actively promoting each sale. The trick is in choosing the right products and platforms, ensuring they align with your brand and audience. Once set up, these links continue to generate revenue with minimal maintenance, turning your digital presence into a 24/7 money-making machine.

Another angle to explore is digital products. These assets, once created, can be sold repeatedly without additional production costs, making them ideal for passive income. Consider ebooks, online courses, or software tools—each represents an opportunity to leverage your expertise or interests. Once you've established a solid creation process, sales can continue indefinitely. The key to success in this area lies in identifying a niche or a specific demand and delivering high-quality content or solutions.

Rental income from digital properties is another promising frontier. While commonly associated with physical real estate, the same principles apply online. Websites or blogs can be rented out to advertisers or other entrepreneurs. It's a model where your existing audience becomes an asset, and you earn revenue from leasing space on your digital platform. Before diving in, however, it's crucial to build a strong and engaged audience, as this increases the value of your digital real estate.

Then there's the world of online ad revenue, a straightforward passive income model if you've accumulated a steady stream of followers or readers. Platforms like Google AdSense allow you to monetize your digital spaces through advertising. The revenue is directly proportional to the amount of traffic your site receives, making traffic generation an essential precursor. While it sounds simple, it requires consistent effort to drive and sustain high levels of engagement.

Many entrepreneurs also find passive income through dividend investing online. By investing in high-yield dividend stocks or funds, you can earn returns without direct management. Though not without risk, a well-researched portfolio can provide a reliable income stream. It requires an understanding of the market and a proactive approach at first, but over time, your investments can generate returns with little continuous effort.

Yet, aspiring entrepreneurs must approach passive income with realistic expectations. It's tempting to buy into promises of instant wealth, but the truth is more grounded. Building these income streams demands dedication, patience, and, most importantly, an understanding of where your efforts are best directed for the greatest long-term gain. Remember, the most successful passive income streams result from combining knowledge, strategy, and perseverance.

In essence, passive income opportunities present a chance to reshape how entrepreneurs think about earning. It's an exciting realm where creativity and strategic planning converge, allowing individuals to maximize their time and resources efficiently. It's about constructing a framework that gradually requires less direct involvement, freeing you to explore new ventures or simply enjoy more of life's moments. The journey to passive income may start with a single step or idea, but its potential knows no bounds.

Automation in Digital Ventures

Embracing the world of digital ventures often means finding ways to streamline operations while maximizing output. Automation stands as a pivotal component in this process, especially for aspiring entrepreneurs looking to create passive income streams. The allure of automation doesn't just lie in its efficiency; it's about liberating your time to focus on scaling your business or pursuing new opportunities. By integrating automated solutions, you can achieve a balance between growing your venture and enjoying the freedom that a passive income promises.

Automation comes in various forms and serves multiple functions across digital ventures. Consider email marketing, a cornerstone for many online businesses. An automated email sequence can nurture leads, engage customers, and even drive sales—all without constant supervision. Imagine setting up a welcome series that introduces newcomers to your offerings, followed by periodic value-packed newsletters that keep them hooked. This level of personalization, enabled by automation, transforms what was once a manual task into a hands-off profit stream.

Moreover, automation isn't exclusive to customer interactions. It can significantly enhance backend processes like inventory management for e-commerce entrepreneurs. Tools that automatically restock products or update listings with the click of a button reduce human error and ensure operational continuity. This seamless transition of inventory from one phase to another not only saves precious time but also boosts customer satisfaction as you maintain consistent stock levels.

A different yet equally potent form of automation is in financial management. Automated invoicing and payment tracking systems ensure that freelance professionals and digital creators get paid promptly. You can set these systems to follow up with clients on overdue invoices without lifting a finger, minimizing awkward conversations and providing consistent cash flow. Such automation frees you from tedious administrative tasks, allowing you to dedicate more energy to creating high-value services or products.

Now, let's delve into content creation automation. If you're a digital entrepreneur running a blog, consider tools that can streamline content curation and social media scheduling. Automated systems can gather trending topics, curate engaging articles, and schedule posts across various platforms. These processes, once arduous, can now be handled with precision, ensuring your online presence remains active even when you're not directly engaged. Automation in this context does more than spare your time—it magnifies your influence.

Of course, with these benefits come some considerations. Automation, while incredibly useful, requires initial investment in terms of both time and resources. It's crucial to choose tools and systems aligned with your business goals. Start with a clear understanding of what you need and how automation can meet those needs. Take the time to research and test different solutions, ensuring they integrate well with existing systems and can scale with your growth.

Furthermore, adopting an automated approach demands a shift in mindset. It's about transitioning from a hands-on mentality to embracing a management role where your priority is setting up and overseeing systems. This strategic pivot will empower you to focus on strategic decision-making, exploring new markets, and enhancing your business's value proposition. Automation can transform your business model by turning repetitive tasks into opportunities for growth and innovation.

Another exciting area where automation can contribute to passive income is in the realm of drop shipping. Automated platforms can handle the entirety of order processing, from customer purchase to supplier notification and shipping, without any manual input. This automation allows drop shipping businesses to operate at scale with minimal operational headaches, making it an attractive model for passive entrepreneurship.

Incorporating automation also involves data analysis. Platforms offering real-time analytics enable entrepreneurs to gain insights while automating data collection and reporting processes. By understanding customer behavior patterns, identifying successful product lines, and tracking performance metrics, businesses can make informed decisions about scaling operations. Through automation, you can continuously refine your approach without dedicating extensive time to analysis.

The empowerment doesn't stop with processes alone; consider customer service. Using automated chatbots can greatly enhance customer interaction, providing instant answers to routine inquiries and freeing up human resources to tackle more complex queries. This ensures that your clients feel heard and valued, which is an essential component of building a loyal customer base. However, balance is key—know when human intervention is necessary and ensure that your automation strategy maintains a personal touch.

Ultimately, the quest for passive income through digital ventures becomes much clearer with automation by your side. It's not about replacing human effort but rather amplifying it. Entrepreneurs who approach automation strategically can unlock a future of consistent revenue streams that grow without perpetual attention. Automation enables more than just efficiency; it fosters creativity, innovation, and the ability to truly scale your business.

As we explore these transformative opportunities, remember that automation is an ever-evolving landscape. Stay abreast of emerging technologies and be adaptable to new trends that can further enhance your business model. Automation is more than a tool; it's a mindset that aligns with the very essence of passive income. Take the leap and harness its potential to ultimately craft a venture that works as seamlessly as possible—and benefit from the fruits of your automated labor.

Revenue Streams Without Constant Attention

In a world that's always on the move, the appeal of revenue streams that don't require constant attention can't be overstated. Imagine having income that flows in while you're asleep, on vacation, or simply enjoying a leisurely Sunday brunch. This concept of "earning while disengaged" isn't just a fantasy—it's a tangible reality for those who learn the art of passive income.

The first step to achieving such financial freedom is to recognize distinct opportunities that generate income without daily intervention. Setting up these revenue streams might require effort and strategic planning upfront, but once established, they can sustain themselves with minimal oversight. Imagine the concept of planting seeds that grow into trees, providing shade and fruit for years with little more than occasional pruning—this is the essence of passive income.

One promising avenue is creating digital products like e-books, templates, or software that meet specific consumer needs. The beauty of digital products lies in their infinite scalability. Once they're created, the same product can be sold repeatedly without additional costs. Platforms such as Amazon Kindle Direct Publishing or Etsy for digital templates offer channels to reach a vast audience.

Consider real estate—but not the brick-and-mortar kind. Instead, look at investing in virtual assets, like domain names or websites. This strategy, akin to digital real estate flipping, involves buying undervalued domains or websites, enhancing their value, and eventually reselling them for a profit. With the digital economy consistently evolving, the demand for internet properties continues to rise, offering significant potential for income with minimal direct management.

Another compelling option is affiliate marketing where one can earn commissions by promoting other people's products or services. The secret lies in building a robust platform—a blog, YouTube channel, or social media presence—and integrating affiliate links naturally into your content. This approach demands upfront work to cultivate an audience but becomes largely self-sustaining over time as the audience engages with your content, clicks through links, and completes purchases.

For those inclined toward teaching, online courses present a lucrative opportunity. Once you've gone through the process of recording instructional videos and setting up course materials, platforms like Udemy or Teachable handle the logistics of course distribution. Course upsells and email marketing campaigns can further enhance earnings, all while you focus on creating more content or relaxing as enrollments increase.

Subscription services are also a sought-after model. By providing exclusive content or services on a recurring basis, creators and entrepreneurs can build a community that pays regularly. Whether it's a Patreon membership for artists or a subscription box service in a niche market, the beauty lies in the predictability of income and the development of a loyal customer base.

The gig economy has further expanded opportunities with micro-tasking platforms like Amazon Mechanical Turk. These platforms allow workers to complete small tasks for payment. While individually, the tasks generate small sums, automation tools can be employed to maximize efficiency, turning these micro-income streams into a significant cash flow without constant attention.

Certain investment vehicles can yield passive returns. Dividend-paying stocks or peer-to-peer lending platforms allow returns to grow over time. These are longer-term plays that require initial capital but can result in a steady income with little direct management once an investment strategy is set.

Despite their allure, it's important to approach passive income streams with realistic expectations. While the concept implies minimal effort, there is often a significant initial investment of time, resources, and ingenuity. Carefully evaluating each opportunity's sustainability and potential risks is key.

Ultimately, the goal is to build a portfolio of diverse, passive income streams. This diversification not only mitigates risk but also creates a resilient financial ecosystem that supports your lifestyle regardless of economic fluctuations or personal time commitments.

In embracing this journey toward self-sustaining income, remember that possibilities are endless. Whether through digital goods, asset investments, or leveraging your unique skills and knowledge, the opportunity to step away from conventional work hours and still earn is within reach. What awaits is not just a stream of revenue, but the freedom to shape your life with intention, pursuing passions, and living with more balance and fulfillment.

Let these ideas spark your imagination and motivate actions that bring long-term change. You've already taken the crucial step by seeking this knowledge. Now, it's time to continue with actionable steps and a commitment to redefining what "work" means in your journey to financial freedom.

Chapter 12: Scaling and Sustaining Your Income Streams

You've laid the groundwork, experimented with different avenues, and even tasted some success. Now comes the exciting challenge of scaling and sustaining those income streams you've worked hard to build. The digital landscape is dynamic and full of endless possibilities, but scaling effectively and sustainably is all about strategy. This chapter is your guide to ensuring your streams of income not only grow but do so in a way that's manageable and long-lasting.

First and foremost, scaling your income streams involves identifying the right growth opportunities. What works for one person may not work for another, and that's perfectly okay. It's essential to keep an analytical mind and continually assess areas of your business or freelance endeavors that show the most promise. Look for patterns in your data. Are certain products, services, or content types more popular than others? Trust the numbers, but don't ignore your instincts.

One key approach is diversifying your offerings. If you have a successful blog, consider creating supplementary e-books, online courses, or exclusive content for subscribers. For freelance professionals, explore retainer agreements with clients to create a steady stream of revenue. By expanding your portfolio of products or services, you will protect yourself against market fluctuations and ensure a more stable income. Diversification isn't just about adding more; it's about adding the right things.

As you broaden your horizons, automation will become your best ally. Automating processes doesn't only save time; it also allows you to focus on scaling efforts and creative pursuits. Whether it's using scheduling tools for social media or setting up automated email funnels for marketing campaigns, the time you free up can be reinvested in exploring new growth avenues. Keep in mind, though, that automation should augment your business—not replace the human touch where it genuinely counts.

Another factor to consider is the strength of your personal brand. As you scale, people will be drawn not only to your offerings but to you as well. Your brand is the story people tell about you when you're not in the room. Make sure it conveys trust, authenticity, and value. Engage sincerely with your audience through social media or other channels, and always be open to feedback. Scaling your income is as much about building lasting relationships as it is about numbers.

Now, let's not forget about optimizing existing operations. Often, by refining what you already have, you can yield significant growth. Examine your current workflows, marketing strategies, and customer interactions. Are there bottlenecks or inefficiencies that could be improved or streamlined? Sometimes, the path to scaling is not through adding more but doing better with what you have.

In addition to scaling, sustaining your income streams requires a mindset geared toward continuous learning and adaptation. The digital world changes rapidly with new platforms and technologies emerging all the time. Keep yourself updated, whether through courses, webinars, or industry news. An informed entrepreneur is an empowered one, ready to pivot and seize new opportunities.

Part of sustaining your income also involves managing risks. Evaluate potential threats to your income streams, whether economic shifts, technological changes, or even personal circumstances. By anticipating these risks and preparing for them, either through savings, insurance, or diversified income sources, you create a safety net that lets you focus on growth without constantly looking over your shoulder.

Remember, growth should be sustainable, and not at the expense of your health and well-being. It's easy to fall into the hustle trap, but true success comes from balance. Make time for rest, for family, and for hobbies outside of work. After all, what's the point of scaling your income if you don't have the bandwidth to enjoy the fruits of your labor?

In conclusion, scaling and sustaining your income streams is less about going after every new trend blindly and more about thoughtful, strategic actions that align with your goals and values. It's about building not only wealth but a fulfilling lifestyle. Embrace both the challenges and opportunities, and you'll find that this journey is as rewarding as it is transformative.

So, take a moment to review where you are right now. Dive into your data, trust your intuition, and don't be afraid to take calculated risks. With persistence and the right strategies, the growth you've been dreaming of is well within your reach.

Analyzing Growth Opportunities

Scaling and sustaining your income streams involves more than just maintaining the status quo. It's about looking ahead and finding new opportunities that can lead to significant growth in your digital ventures. This proactive approach is essential because the online landscape is rapidly changing and full of potential for those willing to explore it. Analyzing growth opportunities means examining your current offerings, understanding audience behavior, and identifying trends that can be leveraged for expansion. By doing so, you can not only sustain your income but potentially scale it to new heights.

To begin, it's crucial to assess your current performance. Understanding what's working and what isn't in your existing plans will give you a clear view of where improvements can be made. Look at data and analytics to evaluate performance indicators such as traffic, conversion rates, and customer engagement. These metrics can tell you where your strengths and weaknesses lie, providing valuable insights into how and where you might expand.

Next, consider market trends and consumer demands. New trends often signify opportunities to grow. Think about how societal shifts, technological advancements, or changes in consumer behavior could impact your business. By staying ahead of these trends, you can position your offerings to meet new demands, potentially reaching untapped segments of your market. Remember, the ability to adapt quickly to these changes can set you apart from competitors who are slower to respond.

One strategy for analyzing growth opportunities is to conduct a SWOT analysis—identifying your Strengths, Weaknesses, Opportunities, and Threats. This exercise, though seemingly simple, can be incredibly revealing. It helps you understand both internal and external factors affecting your digital enterprise. Strengths and opportunities often overlap, leading you to unexplored avenues, whereas acknowledging weaknesses and threats allows you to anticipate hurdles and prepare accordingly.

Another key aspect of growth is diversification. While we've focused on diversifying income streams throughout this book, it's worth reemphasizing its importance when considering growth. Expanding into new areas, whether it's launching a new product line or tapping into different markets, can mitigate risk and create additional channels for revenue. However, diversification should always align with your core competencies and brand, ensuring that any new venture complements your existing offerings.

Moreover, don't overlook feedback from your audience. Customers provide invaluable insights that can uncover areas ripe for growth. Use surveys, social media interactions, and reviews to gather perspectives from your audience. Their feedback can spur innovations and adjustments that resonate more closely with market needs, thereby enhancing growth opportunities.

Collaboration is another fertile ground for growth. Partnering with others lets you leverage joint resources and expertise. Look for potential partnerships that could create a synergy greater than the sum of its parts: businesses with complementary products, influencers with access to your target audience, or even cross-promotional opportunities that increase reach. Such collaborations can open doors to new markets and introduce efficiencies that drive scalable growth.

Practically speaking, start small to test these new growth avenues. When dabbling in new markets or testing products, it's wise to begin with a pilot program or a limited release. This approach reduces risk while allowing you to gather valuable data that can inform larger rollouts. Analyze this data to refine your offerings and strategy, keeping initial failures as learning pivots rather than setbacks.

Technology can also play a pivotal role in enabling growth. From automation tools that streamline processes to analytic platforms that deliver insights at scale, technology is an invaluable partner. Leverage technological solutions to optimize efficiency and free up more time for strategic planning and creative thinking. The more routine tasks are automated or data is streamlined, the more focus you can put into pursuing strategic growth opportunities.

Additionally, focus on building your brand's reputation as a growth strategy. Trust and credibility are currency in the digital economy. Enhancing your brand's reputation can lead to higher customer retention rates and increase your potential customer base through word-of-mouth referrals. A strong reputation can also prepare the soil for introducing new products or services, as a trusted brand can more easily capture and sustain interest.

Finally, remain agile and adaptable. The digital market is fluid, and static plans can quickly become obsolete. Analyzing growth opportunities isn't a one-time activity but an ongoing process. Regular assessments and flexibility will allow you to tweak strategies quickly in response to changes in the market environment. Establishing a culture of continual learning and adaptation will serve you well, ensuring that you are both poised for new growth and resilient against the uncertainties that come with it.

In conclusion, analyzing growth opportunities requires a balanced approach of introspection and outward analysis. By leveraging data, exploring diversification, embracing collaboration, and staying ahead of trends, you can unlock pathways that lead to sustainable growth. The task is dynamic and ongoing, but with diligence and strategic insight, you'll be well-equipped to scale your income streams to new levels of success.

Long-Term Strategies for Sustained Success

Scaling your income streams is an exhilarating journey, one that's packed with possibilities and invigorating challenges. But as you set your sights on the horizon, it's crucial to consider the long-term strategies that will not only support growth but sustain it. It's about planting seeds that will grow strong roots, giving your endeavors a sturdy foundation for years to come.

Consider this: The digital world is forever evolving. What's trending today might be obsolete tomorrow. Therefore, flexibility becomes your best friend. It's paramount to keep a finger on the pulse of industry updates and technological advancements. By remaining adaptable, you'll better position yourself to pivot when necessary, ensuring that your strategies are not only current but ahead of the curve.

One potent strategy for long-term success lies in diversification. While your journey may start with a single income stream, like a blog or an online store, you should continually seek opportunities to augment your portfolio. Diversification isn't about scattering your efforts thin but widening your scope in a calculated manner. For instance, if your primary source of income is a successful online course, consider branching into related areas such as webinars, e-books, or affiliate partnerships that complement your existing content.

Investing in education is another key player in sustained success. Continuous learning should be an integral part of your strategy. Whether it's taking an online course to refine your digital marketing skills or attending webinars on industry trends, staying educated arms you with the tools to navigate the ever-changing online landscape. Remember, the more you know, the more you can adapt and innovate.

Networking can't be underestimated. Building a supportive community around your ventures fosters both growth and sustainability. Engage with fellow entrepreneurs, join relevant online groups, and participate in forums where you can both offer and receive support. By cultivating a network, you'll not only gain insights and advice from those who've walked a similar path but also create opportunities for collaborations that can propel your progress.

While diversification and networking are vital, never lose sight of the importance of authenticity. In a digital arena overflowing with content and commerce, authenticity helps you stand out. All successful entrepreneurs share a common trait: they are genuine. Whether it's through your personal brand, the products you create, or the services you offer, authenticity fosters trust, which in turn cultivates loyalty among your audience. Loyal customers are not only repeat customers but ambassadors who amplify your reach by word of mouth.

Scalability should be a constant consideration in your strategy. How can your current offerings be expanded or improved upon to reach more people without compromising quality? Embrace technologies that automate and enhance your operations. Automation not only enables you to manage resources more efficiently but also frees up time to focus on strategic decisions rather than daily logistics.

Next, the power of analytics. In the digital realm, data is the goldmine. It equips you with insights about your audience and their behavior. Use analytics to track key performance indicators relevant to your income streams. By evaluating what's working and what isn't, you can make evidence-based decisions tailored for sustainable growth.

It's equally important to nurture your mental and physical well-being throughout this journey. The pursuit of long-term success can be draining, so establishing a healthy work-life balance is essential. Regularly assess your workload and ensure that your drive for success doesn't outpace your capacity to handle it. Self-care keeps you at your best, allowing you to remain innovative and enthusiastic.

Lastly, embrace failure as a stepping stone, not a stumbling block. The path to sustained success is rarely linear. Challenges and setbacks are inevitable, but they are also opportunities for learning and growth. Resilience will be your guiding star. Understanding that failure is part of the learning process enables you to bounce back with even greater determination and insight.

In closing, long-term success in scaling and sustaining your income streams is about intertwining strategy with adaptability, education with authenticity, and data-driven decisions with personal well-being. It's about preparing to weave through the tides of change with resilience and vision. Armed with these strategies, you'll be well-equipped to not only reach but maintain the successes you're tirelessly working towards.

Conclusion

Congratulations on reaching the conclusion of this journey. By now, you've explored an array of strategies and insights on building sustainable online income streams. The digital landscape is vast and full of potential, ready to be harnessed by those who approach it with knowledge and determination. As you stand at the threshold of this new venture, remember that the path to financial independence is not only about diversifying income but also about empowering yourself and embracing change.

Every chapter of this book was crafted to guide you through the nuances of creating and maintaining online revenue. From understanding the foundational aspects of the digital world to exploring specific income avenues like blogging, e-commerce, and freelancing, you've acquired a toolkit designed for success. Now, it's up to you to take these tools and build something uniquely yours.

Breaking into the digital economy isn't merely about mastering a single discipline. It demands adaptability—the courage to learn, unlearn, and relearn. And that's a good thing. Flexibility is your ally in this ever-evolving market. By continuously expanding your skills and diversifying your income sources, you not only mitigate risks but also unlock new possibilities. These are opportunities to innovate and grow in ways you might have never imagined.

As you embark on this digital adventure, keep in mind that every successful entrepreneur started where you are right now—at the beginning. It's a point of potential, rich with unexplored opportunities and lessons waiting to be learned. Your journey will be uniquely yours, molded by your passions, strengths, and ambitions. Embrace this individuality, for it is your key differentiator.

Failure might accompany your journey, but it's a seasoned teacher. Each setback is a lesson designed to refine your strategies and strengthen your resolve. Don't let the fear of failure paralyze you.

Instead, let it fuel your hunger for success, steering you toward creative solutions and innovative paths.

Your network will serve as your backbone throughout this endeavor. Building connections with like-minded individuals can lead to collaborative opportunities, sharing experiences, and learning from mentors who have walked a similar path. The relationships you cultivate in the digital world could open doors you never knew existed.

Remember, in this pursuit of online income, sustainability is key. It's not merely about making money—it's about building something that lasts, providing value that continuously resonates with your audience or clients. Focus on delivering quality, cultivating trust, and maintaining a strong online presence.

As you scale your income streams, don't lose sight of the importance of balance—between work and rest, ambition and gratitude. Allowing time for rejuvenation will keep your creativity flowing and your motivation high. After all, the goal is to create a business that serves your life, not the other way around.

Your journey towards building sustainable online income streams is more than a financial mission—it's a journey of personal growth and transformation. You're not just changing your financial status, but you're evolving into a leader in a digital revolution. Embrace this journey with courage, enthusiasm, and an unwavering belief in your potential.

With the knowledge and strategies laid out in these chapters, the digital world is yours to conquer. Go forward with an adventurous spirit, an entrepreneurial mind, and the tenacity to turn your vision into reality. The future of your online success begins now.

May your endeavors be prosperous, your challenges surmountable, and your journey rewarding. Here's to a future brimming with opportunities and the realization of your dreams through sustainable online income. You have all the tools you need—now it's time to build your masterpiece.

Appendix A: Resources for Online Entrepreneurs

Embarking on the journey of online entrepreneurship can feel both exhilarating and daunting. The digital world offers boundless opportunities, but navigating it requires the right tools and knowledge. Here, we'll provide some invaluable resources to help you along the way. These resources are designed to empower your efforts, whether you're just starting or looking to scale your existing ventures.

1. Educational Platforms

First on your entrepreneurial toolkit should be a solid foundation of knowledge. Online learning platforms like **Coursera**, **Udemy**, and **LinkedIn Learning** offer courses on various aspects of digital business—from social media marketing to web development. These platforms allow you to learn at your own pace, making it easier to balance learning with real-world application.

2. Website and E-commerce Tools

Setting up an online presence is crucial for any digital entrepreneur. Platforms like **WordPress** and **Shopify** make it easy to build a professional website or online store. They're user-friendly and come with plenty of tutorials to guide you through the process. Don't overlook tools like **Google Analytics** to track your site's performance and adjust your strategies accordingly.

3. Digital Marketing Resources

In the digital world, visibility is everything. Resources such as the **Google Keyword Planner** and **Ahrefs** can enhance your SEO strategies, while email marketing services like **Mailchimp** can help you maintain engagement with your audience. These tools help ensure your message reaches the right people effectively.

4. Financial Management Software

Understanding your financials is key to sustainable success. Applications like **QuickBooks** and **FreshBooks** offer easy invoicing, expense tracking, and reporting, which are pivotal for maintaining a clear picture of your financial health.

5. Community and Support Networks

No entrepreneur is an island—connecting with others can accelerate your journey. Online forums and communities such as **Reddit's Entrepreneur sub** and **GrowthHackers** offer a platform to seek advice, share experiences, and collaborate. Membership sites like **Startup Grind** provide both inspiration and practical support.

6. Productivity and Organization Apps

Staying organized can vastly improve your efficiency. Apps like **Trello** and **Asana** help manage projects and tasks. Coupled with communication tools like **Slack** and **Zoom**, they keep you and your team connected and productive even at a distance.

These resources represent just a glimpse into the wealth of support available to online entrepreneurs today. While these tools are crucial, remember that the most powerful asset is your willingness to adapt and learn. With these resources at your disposal, you're better equipped to tackle the ever-evolving challenges of the digital business world and ultimately pave your path to success.

Don't miss out!

Visit the website below and you can sign up to receive emails whenever david holman publishes a new book. There's no charge and no obligation.

https://books2read.com/r/B-A-STXT-CHCHF

BOOKS 2 READ

Connecting independent readers to independent writers.

Also by david holman

Riot Survival Guide
Guide To Natural Disasters
ElectroCulture Basics
The Taylor Swift Effect
Athletic Training
Beginners Guide To YOGA
Functional Fitness
Meditation Basics
Surviving Catastrophe In an Urban Enviroment
Urban Gardening Tips And Tricks For Beginners
Applying The Principles Of The Universal Laws
Surviving The Rising Cost Of Everything
Rescue In The Woods
Bruce Lee's Way: The Art Of A Modern Day Warrior
Slayers Creed
The Path Of Jeet Kune Do
How To Be Your Own Doctor
Muscles And Strength Building
Legacy of Preparedness
Chaos To Calm
Life Of Contentment
Streams Of Prosperity